Maynooth College is two hundred years old. Age is honourable and achievement is to be honoured, and both age and achievement will be widely celebrated on the bicentenary. The occasion will see the celebration of Maynooth's original purpose, still continued, the training of priests for Ireland. It will also mark the development of that purpose over two centuries, eventually to include third-level education of men and women in philosophy and theology, in the sciences, and in the arts.

To honour in an appropriate way these two hundred years of teaching, members of the college staff are publishing a series of books in a number of academic disciplines. Edited by members of the College Faculty, these books will range from texts based on standard theology courses to interdisciplinary studies with a theological or religious involvement.

The venture is undertaken with pride in the long Maynooth academic tradition and in modest continuance of it.

GW00401076

LITERATURE AND THE SUPERNATURAL

In memory of
Barbara Hayley
Professor of English
St Patrick's College, Maynooth
1986-1991

Edited by Brian Cosgrove

Literature and the Supernatural

ESSAYS FOR THE MAYNOOTH BICENTENARY

the columba press

First edition, 1995, published by
the columba press
93 The Rise, Mount Merrion, Blackrock, Co Dublin

Cover by Bill Bolger
Origination by The Columba Press
Printed in Ireland by Colour Books, Dublin

ISBN 1 85607 143 X

Contents

Preface

Modernity, according to Julia Kristeva, is to be characterised as 'the first epoch in human history in which human beings attempt to live without religion'. Also implicated in this marginalisation of religion, it seems, is a general suspicion of the metaphysical and the transcendent: partly because an interest in those categories may serve only to distract us from what are felt to be the more urgent programmatic requirements of various ideologies (feminism, for example, or alternative commitments to egalitarianism, acknowledging beyond any attempted mystification the raw workings of power in the cultural formation, and calling for a redistribution of such power). Jane Marcus provides a strikingly explicit version of the bias of our age: writing as an avowedly feminist critic of Virginia Woolf, she confesses that:

> I had avoided the subject of Woolf's mysticism ... feeling that acknowledging her as a visionary was a trap that would allow her to be dismissed as another female crank, irrational and eccentric. I was drawn to her most anti-capitalist, anti-imperialist novels, to Woolf the socialist and feminist ...

Marcus' comment, remarkable for its honesty, is equally remarkable in its representative unease in the face of the mystical and the 'visionary'. (Woolf herself was less inhibited, and her *Collected Essays*, for instance, include pieces on Henry James's ghost stories and on 'The Supernatural in Fiction'.)

The present cultural climate, then, and the current state of literary studies, are not such as to encourage an interest in the 'supernatural': if such an interest is to be justified at all, it will have to take account of prevalent opinion. One can still, however, treat the supernatural, rather as William James treated religion in *The Varieties of Religious Experience*, as an empirically given record of human encounter with that which lies outside the familiar world: without (as James shows) either sceptical prejudgement, or an undue willingness to succumb to the 'mystique' of the supernatural.

Arguably, all of the essays in this collection (by members of the English Department at Maynooth) are suitably cautious in their approach.

The supernatural is here considered as a recurrent literary category which reveals or implicates historically documented cultural formations (as in the pieces by Lucas, Hayes, Morash and Mac Gabhann); or else (as in the essay by Joe Cleary) the writer explores in a related way how the handling of a supernatural theme in contemporary film illuminates, and is illuminated by, current socio-cultural trends. Other essays consider how individual writers exploit established 'codes' relating to supernatural (or supra-natural) experiences, creating from these a prism through which to view their own situation (McGuinness, Denman); or elaborate through available theological systems a sense of problematic situatedness in a *Lebenswelt* to which supernatural belief seems appropriate (Cosgrove).

What the contributors have in common is a reluctance to endorse a belief in the supernatural in its own right (the concern being rather to explore the effects or implications of the supernatural as these are available for documentation, analysis and critique in literature and cultural history): but within that shared attitude the variety of topics is matched by a diversity of approach. The result is a rich kaleidoscope which, it is hoped, is a fitting contribution to the bicentenary celebrations of St Patrick's College, Maynooth.

It is appropriate, finally, to take this opportunity to thank Ms Karen Donovan for her patience, perseverance and commitment in the preparation of the text for publication, and in particular for her willingness to act on her own initiative when circumstances so required.

Brian Cosgrove

Keeping up Appearances:
Chaucer's Franklin
and the Magic of the Breton Lay Genre

Angela M. Lucas

At the beginning of the prologue to his Tale, the Franklin informs his pilgrim audience that he is going to tell a Breton Lay, and even attempts a brief description of the genre. In seeking to discover why Chaucer chose to cause his Franklin to claim a Breton Lay as a source for his Tale, it is necessary to examine his prologue and Tale in the light of what is known about this genre.

With the meaning 'narrative poem' of between one hundred and a thousand lines, the Breton Lay is usually associated with Marie de France. Marie wrote in French in the second half of the twelfth century, probably c.1160-80: though it is likely that she lived in England (Ewert., xv-xvi; Fox 303-6 and 317-26). Her *Lais* have been called *nouvelles en vers*. Though not sung, each poem can nevertheless arguably be thought of as 'lyric', associated with a single sentiment, event, or experience, expressing emotions generally related to love (Stevens; Mickel). Twelve *Lais* are definitely ascribed to Marie, all in British Library MS Harley 978, an Anglo-Norman manuscript dating from the middle of the thirteenth century (Warnke, lx-lxi).

There are also anonymous Lays of the Marie de France type, and it seems likely that Marie was not the first to write this kind of poem (Ewert, xv: Foulet, 'Marie de France', 310-11). However she probably was the first to make such poems from material of Celtic/British origin based on matter which had been used in the making of a certain kind of musical composition by Breton minstrels. In any event she raised the genre to the distinguished position it occupies in medieval literature, and some other Lays are clearly inspired by the same material as that which Marie was using (Bullock-Davies, 28-29).

The production of some Breton Lays in English, such as *Sir Orfeo*, *Sir Degaré*, and *Lay le Freine*, in the late thirteenth and early fourteenth centuries, seemed to give the genre a new impetus for a while. Possibly Chaucer's Franklin's claim that his Tale (composed c.1389) is a Breton Lay may be seen as a reflection of that interest, albeit somewhat late. After the *Franklin's Tale*, an interest in Breton

11

Lays in English is shown in the fifteenth century by such poems as *Emaré*, *The Erle of Tolous*, *Sir Gowther*, and Thomas Chestre's *Sir Launfal*. Although some of these poems deal with material very different in origin from that used by Marie, the interest that they show in the Breton Lay genre may be due in no small measure to the reminder of its existence given by Chaucer in the *Franklin's Tale*.

Marie is quite clear about what she calls a Breton Lay. She says that she is going to *narrate* stories from which Bretons made *lais*:

> Les contes ke jo sai verrais
> Dunt le Bretun unt fait les lais
> Vos conterrai assez briefment. (*Guigemar* 19-21)

In *Lanval* she writes

> L'aventure d'un autre lai
> … vus cunterrai. (1-2)

The Breton *lais* she refers to were musical. The Bretons made a lai of *Guigemar*, for example, *en harpe e en rote* (885). Thus Marie is saying that she is dealing with the same material from which Bretons made musical lays, but she does not claim to be producing the same kind of compositions. Although descriptions of these musical Breton lais to which Marie refers do occur in medieval literature, they are sufficiently imprecise to make it difficult to reconstruct the exact method of performance (Bullock-Davies, 23-24). That explanations of performance were proffered at all – by the poet of the Old French Romance *Horn et Rimenhild* and by Gottfried von Strassburg in his *Tristan* – suggests that the Breton *lai* was considerably more obscure than a *roundel* or a *pastourelle* (Bullock-Davies, 18-19). From *Horn*, from *Tristan*, from the Old Norse prose *Strandar Strengleikr* 'The Lai of the Beach', and from Wace's *Brut*, we learn certain things about these compositions. The original Breton *lai* involved a special kind of musical performance with technical features peculiarly Breton. It seems that it could have been an instrumental piece, without vocal accompaniment. A harp melody alone could carry the title *lai*. Tristan, for example, is able to speak to a harper who is playing a *lai*; evidently the harper cannot be singing (*Tristan* 3520-25; Bullock-Davies, 10). Alternatively a *lai* could have words as well as music: Tristan, again, could perform *lais* in four languages, Breton, Welsh, Latin, and French (*Tristan* 3624-31; Bullock-Davies, 21). However, the distinguishing feature was the music. In *Strandar Strengleikr* a special lai is commissioned by William I of England and he sends his best harpers to the Red Woman of Brittany to learn how to perform it. There does not seem to be any question of words or stanzas; a musical performance is what is required (*Strandar Strengleikr*, 202-

5; Bullock-Davies, 25-26). Marie de France likewise does not mention singing as a component part of the original musical *lais*.

Marie is generally very clear that she is narrating the *conte* or story of an event upon which Breton minstrels had based their musical *lais*. Even in the one instance where she does say that she is composing a *lai*, the real nature of her composition is not in doubt:

Le lai del Freisne vus dirai
Sulunc le cunte que jeo sai. (*Le Fresne*, 1-2)

The *contes* to which Marie refers, and from which Bretons made their *lais*, may or may not have been written down. In the Prologue to her *lais* Marie says that she is going to tell of events which she has heard related:

Plusurs en ai oi conter,
Ne(s) voil laisser ne oblier:
Rimez en ai e fait ditié.
Soventes fiez en ai veillié. (*Prologue*, 39-42)

The suggestion is of an oral tradition, but once, in *Guigemar*, she says she will record the stories (*contes*) *Sulunc la lettre e l'escriture* (23). This statement could be a claim to a written source. Alternatively, it could possibly refer to her own writing down of the story (Foulet, 'Prologue', 71). The application of the term 'Breton Lai' to Marie's narrative poems and to those of her successors arose, quite understandably, from what she herself wrote, and is sanctioned by common usage, but it is not, as can be seen, without ambiguities, for her *Lais* are not the same kind of compositions as those of the Breton minstrels.

The crucial passage in exploring the Breton Lay ascription of the *Franklin's Tale* is the first seven lines of the Franklin's prologue.

Thise olde gentil Britouns in hir dayes
Of diverse aventures maden layes,
Rymeyed in hir firste Briton tonge,
Whiche layes with hir instrumentz they songe
Or elles redden hem for hir plesaunce;
And oon of hem have I in remembraunce,
Which I shal seyn with good wyl as I kan. (709-15)

According to the *Oxford English Dictionary* and the *Middle English Dictionary* the word 'lay' (*Franklin's Tale*, 710) meaning 'narrative poem' is recorded only twice before Chaucer. The first recorded use is in *Sir Orfeo* (c.1330). In fact, the only pre-Chaucerian evidence for narrative Breton Lays in English lies with *Sir Orfeo* and two other poems, *Lay le Freine* and *Sir Degaré*, which are preserved with it in one manuscript, the Auchinleck manuscript, National Library of Scotland, Advocates' MS 19.2.2. In 1941 Loomis argued that Chaucer knew the Auchinleck manuscript and she indicated the similarities between the Franklin's prologue and the prologue to *Lay le Freine* in that manuscript. For this purpose she distinguished the ideas contained in the Franklin's prologue as follows:

(1)   Lays were made by Bretons;
(2)   The Bretons were *gentil*;
(3)   They lived in olden days;
(4)   They composed in their own language;
(5)   The lays were in rhyme;
(6)   The lays were sung;
(7)   The lays were accompanied by musical instruments;
(8)   The lays were written down and could be read;
(9)   The lays were on diverse subjects (Loomis, 'Breton Lays', 18).

She then used this analysis of the first seven lines of the Franklin's prologue to argue that Chaucer knew a great deal about Breton Lays and that this knowledge helped him to produce what she considered the delightful tale of Dorigen's dilemma. Loomis evidently wished to suggest the likenesses between *The Franklin's Tale* and other Breton Lays when she stated that the 'Franklin's prologue remains... the only safe, entirely unquestioned evidence of what Chaucer knew, or thought he knew, about Breton Lays' (Loomis, 'Breton Lays', 19). Her premise excludes the possibility that what we are told in the Franklin's prologue represents the limits only of the knowledge attributed to the Franklin by Chaucer. In fairness to Loomis, it should perhaps be noted that critical awareness of the need to differentiate between an author's own narratorial voice and that of his fictional narrator was not then generally recognised, a development in Chaucerian studies that probably received its greatest impetus from the appearance of Donaldson's 1954 article distinguishing Chaucer the Poet from Chaucer the Pilgrim, neither of whom were the same as Chaucer the Man.

The prologue to *Lay le Freine* in the Auchinleck manuscript is a key source of information on English Breton Lays. This prologue is also found as a prologue to *Sir Orfeo* in the two other, later, versions of that Lay (in British Library MS Harley 3810, and Oxford Bodleian Library MS Ashmole 61: see Bliss, *Sir Orfeo* edition). Possibly *Sir Orfeo* in the Auchinleck version also used these lines, but this conclusion must remain uncertain as the leaf containing the end of *Sir Tristram* and the beginning of *Sir Orfeo* is now missing (Bliss, 'Sir Orfeo 1-46'). The *Le Freine/Orfeo* prologue contains the most detailed account in English of the Breton Lay.

> We redeth oft & findeth [y-write]
> & this clerkes wele it wite,
> Layes that ben in harping
> Ben y-founde of ferli thing:
> Sum bethe of wer & sum of wo,
> & sum of ioie & mirthe al-so,
> & sum of trecherie & of gile,
> Of old auentours that fel while,
> & sum of bourdes & ribaudy,
> & mani ther beth of fairy;
> Of al thinges that men seth
> Mest o loue, for sothe, thai beth.
> In Breteyne this layes were wrought,
> [First y-founde & forth y-brought,
> Of Auentours that fel bi dayes,
> Wher-of Bretouns maked her layes.]
> When kinges might our y-here
> Of ani meruailes that ther were,
> Thai token an harp in gle & game
> & maked a lay & yaf it name. (1-20)

Having argued that Chaucer knew the Auchinleck manuscript, Loomis summed up by saying that,

> the Auchinleck prologue accounts for everything that Chaucer actually says and we have no reason for going beyond his own statements. To all intents and purposes the Franklin's prologue is simply a suavely charming summary of the earlier passage (Loomis, 'Breton Lays', 18 and 24).

While it is difficult to argue with Loomis's main findings – that Chaucer's knowledge of the Breton Lay could have come most easily from the Auchinleck Manuscript – it is important to 'go beyond' Chaucer's Franklin's statement.

To say that Bretons composed lays of *diverse aventures* is not to convey a great deal of information about their contents: it could be true of any body of poetry, lyric or narrative, in the Middle Ages. It is also fairly safe to say that Bretons composed in their own language (Beston, 329), though for a lay to be called 'Breton' it did not have to be in that language if one remembers Tristan's competence in no less than four languages. The statement that they sang their lays *with hir instruments* is also rather vague. The *Le Freine/Orfeo* prologue specifies the harp (19) and Marie also mentions the harp

(*Guigemar*, 885). The harp features in *Horn* and *Tristan*, and in *Strandar Strengleikr*. Wace's Brut speaks of *lais de notes*,

> Lais de vieles, lais de rotes,
> Lais de harpes, lais de frestels. (10547-49)

Moreover, the Franklin immediately undermines his seemingly factual statement that the lays were sung with another:

> Or elles redden hem for hir pleasaunce. (713)

What knowledge we have of the original Breton *lais* suggests that they were for musical performance, in some cases without any words at all. Certainly there is no mention of their being read. The *contes*, which Marie speaks of as her raw material, might have been written down, though one has the impression of an oral tradition, as they were the raw material for the Breton minstrels as well. The Franklin thus alludes to alternative methods of performing a Breton Lay, playing or reading, without actually differentiating between them. He blurs the distinction between the oral/musical *lais* of the Breton minstrels and the short narrative romances of the Marie de France type, also called Breton *Lais*. He is made to attribute both kinds of *lai* to the *olde Britouns* contrary to the evidence of Marie (Foulet, 'Prologue', 707). There seems to be an element of confusion here.

Even were we to assume that Chaucer did not know the tradition within which Marie was working and which she extended so successfully (and there is no way of proving either his knowledge or his ignorance), but did know the *Le Freine/Orfeo* prologue as found in the Auchinleck manuscript, it is still difficult to see how such confusion as that attributed to the Franklin could have arisen. A distinction is made by the poet of the *Le Freine/Orfeo* prologue:

> We redeth oft and findeth (y-write),
> & this clerkes wele it wite,
> Layes that ben in harping
> Ben y-founde of ferli thing. (1-4)

Lines 3-4 are a noun clause object, so that *Layes* (3) is not the direct object of *y-write* or *redeth* (1):

> We read and find written [statements to the effect] that lays that are of harping are found with wondrous subject-matter.

This interpretation is clearer in the early fifteenth-century text of *Sir Orfeo* in MS Harley 3810:

> We redyn ofte & fynde y-w[ryte],
> As clerkes don vs to wyte,
> The layes that ben of harpying
> Ben y-founde of frely thing. (1-4)

The late fifteenth-century text of *King Orfew* in MS Ashmole 61 contains a two-line précis of lines 1-4 which bears out the present interpretation of them:

> The Brytans, as the boke seys,
> Off diuerse thingys thei made ther lays. (7-8)

Thus, it seems fairly safe to say that the English had preserved the idea that information about Breton lays was written down, but not the lays themselves. The *Le Freine/Orfeo* prologue continues by describing the subject-matter of the lays in some detail. Then, while informing us that musical *lais* were composed by Bretons about *auentours*, the author says that he is going to tell one of *this auentours*.

> Now, of this auentours that weren y-falle
> Y can tel sum, ac nought alle:
> Ac herkneth, lordinges [that beth trewe],
> Ichil you telle [Sir Orfewe]. (21-24)

So the *Le Freine/Orfeo* prologue, here cited in the *Sir Orfeo* version, preserves the distinction between a musical lay and the narrative of an *auentour*, just as Marie de France did. A close reading of the *Le Freine/Orfeo* prologue can yield no other interpretation. That this view prevailed is confirmed by the author of the fifteenth-century narrative poem *Sir Gowther*, who made no mistake about the relation of his poem to its supposed Breton source:

> A lai of Bretayn long ysoght
> And owt therof a tale have broght
> That lufly is to tell. (28-30)

He also states:

> This is wreton in parchemyn
> A story bote gud and fyn
> Out of a lai of Breteyne. (685-87; see Donovan, 227).

Thus the Franklin's notion of alternatively reading or singing the same composition is idiosyncratic. No other poem in English claiming to be a Breton lay makes such a claim. It is scarcely possible to ascertain whether the Franklin's statement represents Chaucer's understanding or not, but to imagine a naïve Chaucer, uninformed even by fourteenth-century English standards of the facts about Breton Lays, is to stretch the imagination a good deal. Lowes thought that the 'fundamental difficulty about the Breton lay is that we have only Chaucer's word for it' (727). In fact we have only the Franklin's word for it. The Franklin's prologue is, to re-cast Loomis' finding, a 'safe unquestioned piece of evidence' as to what the

Franklin is revealed to know about Breton Lays, and can be attributed safely only to the Franklin. The Franklin goes on to make it clear that he is going to tell a *lay*, and not an *aventure*, thus further glossing over the distinction drawn by Marie de France and by the anonymous poet of the *Le Freine/Orfeo* prologue in the Auchinleck manuscript (cf Foulet, 'Prologue', 707).

As there is no Celtic or Breton analogue for the *Franklin's Tale*, and the story is evidently based on a story in the *questioni d'amore* episode in Boccaccio's *Il Filocolo*, the prologue to the *Franklin's Tale* is of major importance for the argument that the Tale is a Breton Lay (Loomis, 'Breton Lays', 18-19; Bryan and Dempster, 377-83). So we have a situation where the *Franklin's Tale* is considered to be a Breton Lay primarily because the Franklin says it is. Having begun to throw doubt on the accuracy of his claim from the statements in his prologue, we have to look now at the reasons why this specific genre is imposed on his *Tale*, and we have to look at the *Tale* itself to see if it lives up to the claim made for its genre by the narrator.

The Franklin's stated belief that the *Britouns* who made *layes* were *gentil* ('aristocratic') has sometimes been attributed to the fact that the *Le Freine/Orfeo* prologue says that they were made by *kinges*, though the *Sir Orfeo* prologue in MS Ashmole 61 says that Bretons made their lays about *kyngys* (22-23). However, it is possible to see the Franklin's *gentil Britouns* in the context of his concern for *gentillesse* ('aristocratic behaviour') shown in his words to the Squire (V(F), 682-94). He shows the concern of a rich free man who is not a member of the aristocracy, as is the Squire, whose Tale the Franklin has just interrupted. The Host's forceful rejection of the Franklin's notion of aristocratic etiquette – *Straw for youre gentillesse* (695) – comes immediately before the Franklin launches into his little account of *gentil Britouns* and their Lays. The Franklin may have been made to conceive of the *olde … Britouns* as *gentil* because their nobility could be made to reflect his apparent understanding of a cultural activity supposedly fitted for noble people, an understanding which the Host's remark has just called in question. It seems to be an accepted part of the history of the narrative lays that the term Breton Lay was applied to many short narrative poems not derived from Breton sources in order to enhance their appeal. Writers found it advantageous 'to call any short narrative poem of a serious nature a Breton Lay regardless of its source' (Donovan, 100). The Middle English poems *Sir Gowther*, *Emaré*, and *The Erle of Tolous* probably fall into the category of poems called Breton Lays in order to enhance a claim to be thought 'old and therefore bound to be good'.

Yet it might seem implausible, even distasteful, to some critics that Chaucer should employ such a device: the *Franklin's Tale* is, after all, a fine poem that does not need to be bolstered in that way. This problem is overcome if we understand Chaucer the poet causing his character the Franklin to use that device in order to enhance the story he has been called upon to tell, so as to convince his audience of pilgrims of his *gentillesse* and of the superiority of his taste in literature. It must never be forgotten that the *Franklin's Tale* is a narrative within a narrative, and that Chaucer must be consciously at work in causing the Franklin to call his Tale a Breton Lay. There is, as Hart said, ample evidence that Chaucer was conscious of the dramatic situation (109). The inaccuracies of the 'Breton Lay' prologue may thus be attributed to the Franklin. They reveal pretensions to, rather than real knowledge of, the Breton Lay genre. The prologue – and the Tale too – is in effect a reply to Harry Baily's goading remark: *Straw for youre gentillesse!*

A reading of the *lais* of Marie de France and the English Breton Lays of the Auchinleck Manuscript would certainly lead us to expect a Breton Lay to have a prologue, yet the Franklin's prologue only succeeds in sowing doubts as to what is to follow. The earlier examples of the genre would also lead us to expect a Tale which deals with wondrous subject-matter (the *ferli thing* of *Sir Orfeo*, 4). *Sir Orfeo* tells us that *many ther beth of fairy* (10). Breton Lays may be of war, of woe, joy and mirth, treachery or guile (5-7), but

> Of al thinges that men seth,
> Mest of loue, for-sothe, thai beth. (11-12)

Such a Tale may include an exotic but vague setting, subject matter that includes rash promises and impossible tasks, the incorporation of magical beings and events into the 'real' world of the tale, and of course a love-relationship which is subject to trials as well as joys (see Smithers, 61 ff.). It is instructive to look at the *Franklin's Tale* with such points in mind.

(a) The Setting

The setting in Brittany does not necessarily give the *Franklin's Tale* authenticity as a Breton lay. Only one other English Breton lay has a Breton setting, *Lay le Freine*. Of Marie's *Lais* seven have a Breton setting, five do not. A setting in Brittany is as natural (though in this case inaccurate) an assumption about Breton lays as that which assumes that Bretons composed only in the Breton tongue. There is no locale in Brittany which fits the setting of the Franklin's Tale perfectly, although considerable attention is given by the teller to details of geography (P.J. Lucas, 'Setting in Brittany', 19-21). The 'locale' of the Tale is made up of the rocks around the Pointe de Penmarch which exist, and the cliffs which do not. The attention to detail may be a reflection of the character and interests of the Franklin, as he is made to locate events clearly and precisely, and explain them as fully as possible. However such a clearly visualised setting with considerable topographical detail and its apparent precision is not usually found in a Breton Lay.

(b) The Rash Promise

The rash promise motif, which in the *Franklin's Tale* concerns *trouthe* ('fidelity to one's sworn word'), can be used to provide parallels with other Breton Lays and indeed other romances in general. The concept of *trouthe* in the *Tale* has rather a wider scope than the rash promise element (Gaylord, 331-65; Gray, 213-224), but for the moment I want to concentrate on the rash promise alone. Two examples are given by Bryan and Dempster (393): The *Erl of Tolous* and *Sir Tristrem*. In *The Erl of Tolous* a follower of the Empress promises her to an enemy. Though the Empress does not make the promise herself, the promise is adhered to, lest the follower lose his soul. The contrast between this situation and that of Dorigen is considerable: Dorigen makes her own promise and it is never adhered to. In *Sir Tristrem* King Mark promises a minstrel to give him whatever he asks. When the harper asks for Mark's wife Ysonde, the king, after taking advice, lets her go. Mark's unconditional promise is truly rash, and it is the means whereby Ysonde and her lover Tristrem are reunited. Though Mark and Ysonde are 'wed', Ysonde has substituted her maid on the wedding night, and so their relationship is quite different from that of Dorigen and her husband Arveragus in the Franklin's Tale. Tristrem and Ysonde are lovers, and so their relationship is quite different from that of Dorigen and her would-be lover Aurelius. *Sir Orfeo* also contains a rash promise. The fairy king makes a promise to Orfeo to give him whatever he asks. Orfeo asks for his dear wife, Heurodis, who had been taken from him against her will (467-68). The king's serious but unconditional promise is kept, and is the means of reuniting husband and wife.

When looked at closely, Dorigen's promise to Aurelius does not resemble any of the foregoing:

'Aurelie', quod she, 'by heighe God above,
Yet wold I graunte yow to been youre love,
Syn I yow se so pitously complayne,

> Looke what day that endelong Britayne
> Ye remoeve all the rokkes, stoon by stoon,
> That they ne lette shipe ne boot to goon –
> I seye, whan ye han maad the coost so clene
> Of rokkes that ther nys no stoon ysene,
> Thanne wol I love you best of any man,
> Have heer my trouthe, in al that evere I kan.' (989-98)

This apparent agreement to love Aurelius subject to his fulfilling certain specific conditions is sandwiched between two clear refusals. The first would wither the *corage* of the staunchest courtly lover:

> 'By thilke God that yaf me soule and lyf
> Ne shal I nevere been untrewe wyf
> In word ne werk, as fer as I have wit;
> I wol been his to whom that I am knyt.
> Taak this for fynal answere as of me.' (983-87)

It is only after this statement that she adds her 'promise' *in pley* (988). Her second refusal is in reply to Aurelius' question: '*Is there noon oother grace in yow?*' (999):

> 'For wel I woot that it shal never bityde.
> Lat swiche folies out of youre herte slyde.
> What deyntee sholde a man han in his lyf
> For to go love another mannes wyf,
> That hath hir body whan so that hym liketh?' (1001-5)

Dorigen has in fact couched her 'promise' in terms the conditions of which make it look like a playful refusal. Even had it been seriously made, its conditions are never fulfilled by either party. Dorigen does not love Aurelius *best of any man*. She goes to Aurelius because her husband commands her, and not from desire. Arveragus appears to believe that a temporary loan of Dorigen will meet her 'obligation' towards Aurelius, whereas a loan does not fulfil the 'promise' contained in the words she spoke to the young squire. The complexities in this situation are unlike anything to be found in Breton Lays. Aurelius' approach to dealing with the Dorigen's conditions are best dealt with under the headings of Magic and the Impossible Task.

(c) Magic

Magic in the Franklin's Tale is hardly in accordance with normal Breton Lay usage (Hart, 214-16). In Breton Lays marvellous events are either accomplished by fairy beings or they simply occur without explanation. In *Sir Degaré, Sir Orfeo,* and *Sir Launfal,* beings from the fairy world hold equal status with people in the 'real' world of the poem. A relationship is possible between fairy characters and mortal characters in *Sir Degaré* and *Sir Launfal*, also in Marie's *Yonec and Lanval*. It is possible for mortals to penetrate into the world of faery and vice versa. The thoroughly medieval, university-trained and mortal clerk-magician of the *Franklin's Tale*, whose power is based on book-learning, is foreign to the spirit of the Breton Lays that survive in English and French. The contradiction between the employment of the clerk-magician and the Franklin's condemnation of his astrological 'art' as *hethen* (1293) may be seen as stemming from the Franklin's own apparent uncertainty about the reception of his Tale. At one and the same time he both voices his disbelief in magic as *hethen* and anti-Church, and makes his magician a down-to-earth, business-like, professional member of the medieval Church (A. Lucas, 'Astrology', 15; also Hume, 370).

Such magic as the clerk is presented as working is furthermore undermined in two ways. First, his activities are linked to illusions *swiche as thise subtile tregetoures pleye* (1141). Loomis long ago showed that 'tregetoures' were *artisans méchaniques* who produced their magical tricks by means of sleight of hand and mechanical devices ('Secular Dramatics', 242-55). Creating court entertainments such as are described as being within the power of the clerk of Orleans – a barge rowing upon water, flowers growing, a castle appearing and then disappearing, or of knights jousting or ladies dancing – fell within the domain of the medieval architect-engineer and may well have come to Chaucer's attention during his time as clerk of the king's works. Twice the term 'voided' is used in the Franklin's Tale to indicate the conclusion of such magical presentations (1150 and 1195). This is a word 'often used in a specific theatrical sense meaning "hiding completely from the audience"' (Braswell, 106). The word is also used by Aurelius' brother to indicate the effect he wishes the clerk-magician to achieve:

> For with an apparence a clerk may make,
> To mannes sighte, that alle the rokkes blake
> Of Britaigne weren yvoyded everichon. (1157-59).

The second way in which the clerk's activities are undermined is by the suggestion that all he has actually done at the coast of Brittany is to calculate the arrival of a winter high tide, as it is the *colde frosty seson of Decembre* when every lusty man cries *'Nowel'* (1244 and 1255). The verb *semed*, used to describe the clerk's effect upon the rocks, is also used to describe the effects of *tregetoures'* tricks (1296, 1146 and 1151, Bleeth, 120).

Presenting magic and the clerk magician in this way takes the events in the *Franklin's Tale* a very long way from the episode in *Guigemar* (676), in which a lady who needs to escape from her prison discovers that the door of the prison is miraculously open, or to the episode in *Yonec* (336-40) where the pregnant heroine has to escape by leaping nimbly through an impossibly high window, but gives birth to her lover's baby in the fullness of time. The book-learned, university-trained clerk-magician of Orleans' attempts at *tregetoures'* tricks and astrological magic remove the magical element in the Tale as far as possible from the romance of the Breton Lay.

(d) The Impossible Task
In the *Franklin's Tale*, astrological magic is invoked because no attempt is made by Aurelius to carry out to the letter the task set for him by Dorigen. Aurelius does not remove the black rocks *stoon by stoon* (993). He regards their removal as utterly impossible from the start:

'Madame,' quod he, 'this were an inpossible!' (1009)
At first he appears to accept that Dorigen's 'playful' rash promise contains a real refusal of his advances which sees in the *grisly rokkes blake* (859) a permanence equal to the 'unshakeable *trouthe* of her marriage vow'. Yet he quickly falls prey to the illusion that the removal of the rocks by whatever means will bring her to him (Bleeth, 118). His prayer to Phoebus Apollo and his sister, the moon-goddess Lucina, for a miracle (1031-79) indicates his belief in the need for supernatural intervention. Had the rocks disappeared at this point it would have been a truly marvellous occurrence, but they do not. Yet even the so-called 'miracle' he requests is for a perfectly rational change in the movements of two heavenly bodies, as their workings were then understood. He invokes the sun to beg his sister (the moon)

... that she go
No faster cours than ye thise yeres two.
Then shal she been evene atte fulle alway,
And spryng flood laste bothe nyght and day. (1067-70)
Aurelius believes that the same spring-tide could last for two years if the moon kept a uniform pace with the sun, revolving around the earth once a year and not every twenty-eight days. (Chaucer and his contemporaries believed that both sun and moon revolved around the earth.) In this way the rocks would not be taken away but would be hidden from sight. As an alternative, he would like

Lucina to arrange for the rocks to sink into the dark region where *Pluto dwelleth inne* (A. Lucas, 'Astrology', 6-7). Apollo's silence here suggests the view that supernatural intervention is not to be looked for in this Tale (Bleeth, 118). When Aurelius invokes the magical assistance of the clerk-magician of Orleans to make the rocks appear to disappear, it reinforces the view that the only 'magic' in the Tale will be the natural magic of the clerk, and that Aurelius himself is under a greater illusion as to the feasibility of attaining Dorigen's love than any that can be wrought by this learned clerk.

> But thurgh his magik, for a wyke or tweye,
> It semed that alle the rokkes were aweye. (1295-96)

In Marie's *lai, Les Deus Amanz*, on the other hand, a difficult task is set by a king for the would-be suitors of his daughter. Several suitors attempt – and fail – to carry the princess to the top of a high mountain. However, when her lover seeks to make the attempt, the princess decides to have recourse to a strength-potion (something not contemplated in the *Franklin's Tale*). She sends him to her aunt, a student of medicine for more than thirty years who lives at Salerno, a famous centre of medical learning in the Middle Ages. There is apparently no suggestion of witchcraft or magic in the aunt's skills. The lovers are seeking 'medicine' (99), a practical and medieval solution to the problem. For the two lovers, however, the 'magic' resides not in the potion but in the power of love itself, for at the last moment the young man scorns to use the potion, such is the power of his love. Aurelius's feeble attempts to carry out Dorigen's demand compare not at all with the young man's desire in *Les Deus Amanz* to succeed by the strength born of his own love alone. Aurelius does nothing himself, except fetch the clerk-magician, and even that he does only at his brother's behest. Moreover, he is not Dorigen's acknowledged lover, whereas in *Les Deus Amanz* the young man is the princess's chosen lover. Marie's two young lovers together invoke medieval science in order to deceive the girl's father. Aurelius, by employing the clerk to create an *apparence*, seeks to deceive his beloved object, a truly unnatural phenomenon in the ranks of medieval lovers. Chaucer thus uses the motif of the impossible task in a unique way in the Franklin's Tale. There is nothing similar with which it may usefully be compared, as the impossible task was quite different in Chaucer's source in Boccaccio (Bryan and Dempster, 377-97).

(e) The Love-Triangle Situation

Some attempts have been made to fit the *Franklin's Tale* into a

Breton Lay mould by comparing its story-pattern with those of known examples of the genre, especially those of Marie de France. Three Breton Lays whose 'triangle' plots have been compared with that in the *Franklin's Tale* are *Le Fresne*, *Eliduc* and *L'Ombre*. In *Lai de l'Ombre* the lady refuses the lover, but he accepts her decision with such *courtoisie* that she reverses her decision. However, the decision was a relatively simple one of whether or not to love one particular man without further complications, and does not bear direct comparison with the *Franklin's Tale*. In *Lai le Fresne* the heroine's generous gesture in giving up her lover has been compared with Arveragus's generosity in letting Dorigen go to Aurelius. Le Fresne's heroine patiently accepts her lover's marriage and generously decorates the marriage-bed with her silken cloth, the cloth which leads to her being recognised. However, this generous gesture is uncomplicated by a marriage relationship between the lovers. No indissoluble marriage-bond must be broken (as would be the case of the Franklin's Tale) to take the prince away from Le Fresne. She can 'give him up' to marriage with another in a gesture which seems proper, as well as noble and generous. In *Eliduc* the marriage of Eliduc is set aside so that he can marry his young love Guilliadun. His wife's decision coincides with that of the lovers. It is important to note that Eliduc and Guilliadun are lovers, and that both parties to the marriage are agreed on the arrangement. In the Franklin's Tale Aurelius and Dorigen are not lovers. Dorigen makes it clear that she loves her husband. Their marriage-vows are explained with great fullness in the *Franklin's Tale* (Lucas and Lucas, 501-4), a situation unlike that of any known Breton Lay. Arveragus's decision to send his loyal wife to Aurelius is arbitrary: Dorigen clearly does not wish to be released from her marriage vow. She wishes only to be *an humble trewe wyf in word and werk* (758 and 985). There are no divisions, real or imaginary, in her attitude towards Arveragus.

Aurelius is never more than a suitor or suppliant: he is not her lover. Dorigen does not want him. Only in her desire to be *an humble trewe wyf* does she submit to her husband's lordly command to go and commit adultery. Had Dorigen really wanted Aurelius, as Eliduc wanted Guilliadun, then Arveragus's gesture might have been considered generous. It would still not be comparable with the situation in Eliduc, where one relationship is coming to an end and thus allowing another to begin. The same is true of the situation in *Lai le Fresne*. Arveragus, on the other hand, would seem to intend merely to 'loan' Dorigen to Aurelius in the garden. No other exam-

ples of this kind of licence are to be found in the romance fiction of
the Breton Lay genre, and it would undoubtedly have been looked
on askance in fourteenth-century England, so it is difficult indeed
to argue in favour of widespread tolerance. It seems peculiar to the
Franklin. It is not possible to accept Hume's argument, therefore,
that 'by having invoked the Breton lai form, the Franklin is, in
essence, citing precedents for his story'. There is no Breton Lay
which 'sanctions the sort of departures from strict Christian morality
which his plot demands' (Hume, 377).

The husband in Boccaccio's *Il Filocolo* who gets himself into the
only muddle analogous to that of Arveragus is adjudged to be
unwise (Rajna, *Origini;* Bryan and Dempster, Sources, 377-97; Miller,
121-35; Havely, 154-61). It is not, as suggested by Hume, because an
English audience would not take the plot of the *Franklin's Tale* as
casually as did Boccaccio's audience that it has to be dressed up as a
Breton Lay (379). The judgement in Boccaccio is not at all casual.
The husband was generous to give away his wife, but he also gave
away his honour, which was less than wise, the action of a generous
fool in fact (Gaylord, 361). Chaucer cannot be concerned with a possible shocked English reaction to Italian-style immorality. The
author of the Miller's and Reeve's Tales can hardly be concerned
with his English audience's refinement of sensibility. In fact there is
only one candidate to whom responsibility for the evident uneasi-
ness about the way the *Franklin's Tale* is developing can be attributed: the Franklin himself. His apparent unease about the proposed
adultery is shown quite plainly:

> Paraventure an heep of yow, ywis,
> Wol holden hym a lewed man in this,
> That he wol putte his wyf in jupartie.
> Herkneth the tale er ye upon hire crie. (1493-96)

Even the Franklin himself apparently perceives that his plot is
potentially heading for moral disaster. There would seem to be no
reason to call attention to Arveragus's behaviour at this moment
(especially as he is going to be made to live happily ever after with
Dorigen) unless it is to point to the truth: Arveragus's behaviour is
insensitive to Dorigen's stated wishes and feelings, and ignores
both his and her marriage promises. He cares only for outward
appearance. On pain of death (1481) he commands her,

> To no wight telle thou of this aventure (1483)

The Franklin's little aside (1493-96) actually draws attention to
Arveragus's folly and utter lack of *gentillesse*, for he attempts to cat-
egorise Arveragus's action as generous, and so *gentil*, while totally

submerging the folly and sin of his un-*trouthe* towards Dorigen. Lines 1493-96 make it clear that Chaucer the poet is most certainly not glossing over either the improbabilities in the plot nor the evident shortsightedness of his Franklin. He is drawing attention to them. So much for the idea that Chaucer called the *Franklin's Tale* a Breton Lay in order to lose us in the illogicalities of a romance triangle.

(f) Love
The *Le Freine/Orfeo* prologue in the Auchinleck manuscript tells us regarding Breton Lays that

> Mest o love for sothe thai beth. (12)

The *Lais* of Marie de France have been described as extolling the power and value of love (Stevens, 3 ff.). Her *Lais* have also been analysed as indicating different kinds of love, and exploring different aspects of the nature of love itself (Mickel, 41). It is instructive to attempt to see the *Franklin's Tale* in such company and in the company of the English Breton Lays of the early fourteenth century. Love is powerful through obstacles and through time, in *Milun, Guigemar, Emaré,* and *Sir Orfeo*; it defies concealment in *Yonec*; it courts revelations in *Lanval* and *Sir Launfal*; it attempts the impossible in *Les Deus Amanz*. It does not equate with marriage, but it can lead to marriage. It can occur within marriage, as in *Sir Orfeo*; it can be generous and charitable, as in *Lay le Fresne*; it can be adulterous as in *Yonec*; it can be selfish and lustful as in *Equitan*. Love can ennoble in its emphasis on loyalty and consideration, it can be immoderate even when seeking the happiness of another and not the self. Love can lead to terrible suffering.

The *Franklin's Tale* presents a 'triangle' situation and so, on the face of it, arguably resembles Marie's *Eliduc, Yonec,* or *Guigemar*. However, there are important differences. The relationship between Dorigen and Arveragus is observed in great detail. They are husband and wife, but in no conventional way. They have been lovers and the Franklin informs us that Arveragus is willing that they should continue as if they were lovers after their marriage. Arveragus is to be *servant in love and lord in mariage* (793). Whatever else is said to happen between the characters in the Franklin's narrative must be set against the solemn marriage agreement between Dorigen and Arveragus (Lucas and Lucas, 501-3).

At first sight Aurelius, the squire, would appear to be the external threat to the lover's relationship that appears in some Breton Lays. The queen threatens the lovers in *Lanval* and *Sir Launfal*, the father poses a threat in *Les Deus Amanz*, the husband in *Yonec*, the fairy king in *Sir Orfeo*. A problem arises here in that from Aurelius's point of view Arveragus is the obstacle to achieving Dorigen's love. Aurelius loves Dorigen and would woo her away from her sworn husband whom she loves. Already we have a situation of double threat which, by the standards of genuine Breton Lays, is uncharacteristically complicated. The *grisly rokkes blake* (859) which Dorigen requires Aurelius to remove as her condition, albeit in pley (988), of loving him *best of any man* (997) are conceived as an obstacle to love, but, in keeping with the doubly complicated threat just mentioned, the nature of the obstacle shifts according to the point of view. For Dorigen the rocks initially threaten her marriage, because they could prevent Arveragus from travelling home in safety. But when she makes their removal a condition for loving Aurelius, then she has perceived the rocks as having a stability equivalent to her marriage (Owen, 253; Bleeth, 118). At this point the rocks become an obstacle for Aurelius in pursuit of his lady love. Here again the complexity involved in the threatening situation is uncharacteristic of Breton Lays.

Aurelius, under the illusion that the rocks pose the real threat to the achievement of his lady, uses the clerk-magician to deceive Dorigen, and turns the rocks into a threat to the marriage of Dorigen and Arveragus once again. Aurelius's deception alone would not have succeeded, however, had not Arveragus interpreted very literally the text of Dorigen's promise to Aurelius, and ignored the marriage *trouthe* which he and Dorigen had plighted to each other. Therein lies the real threat to the stability of the marriage relationship (Gray, 222). Dorigen's *trouthe* made *in pley* to Aurelius could have no validity in the face of her marriage vow (Gaylord, 350-56). In 'lending' her to Aurelius, Arveragus is not honouring Dorigen's *trouthe* to Aurelius, nor is he honouring his own marriage vow. There is no Breton Lay in existence which involves such a complicated plot of apparently contrary *trouthes* and where the stability of the love relationship is threatened from within rather than without. The complexities and ironies of the narrative remove the *Franklin's Tale* from any place beside known Breton Lays. As for extolling the power and value of love, the *Franklin's Tale* can hardly qualify for such categorisation, containing as it does a would-be suitor who happily practises deceit on his lady, and a husband who can threaten a stable marriage by commanding his wife to commit adultery. Love and the happiness of the beloved cannot be seen as the wellspring of action in the narrative. Dorigen alone maintains her *trouthe* to Arveragus, obeying him like *an humble trewe wyf* (758), even to the point of moral absurdity. She is the victim of deceit and coercion practised on her by two men whom the Franklin is made to try and present as being in love with her. As he is presented to us by the words attributed to him, the Franklin appears to have no conception of the nature of the love he is made to attempt to deal with, nor indeed any true conception of the various aspects of the genre to which he claims his Tale belongs.

It has been suggested that in the *Franklin's Tale* we have a 'hierarchical matching of social status and literary status' (Johnston, 158). Keen to emulate his social betters the Knight and the Squire, the Franklin tells a tale which might be called, in general terms, a romance, but not a romance such as the Knight or Squire have told. It is a 'tale in an associated genre of more modest dimensions, suited to his old-fashioned, romantic tastes' (Johnston, 159). Hart, with different emphasis and results, saw the Franklin 'as ... conscious of his "almost baronial dignity"' (186). It is the 'almost' in this assessment which looms larger than Hart assumed, and which provides the tensions which lie at the centre of the *Franklin's Tale*. The Franklin may be almost an aristocrat, but he has not yet arrived at that social level. Loomis suggested that Breton Lays in English were 'somewhat out of date and fashion' in the latter half of the fourteenth century, as there is no manuscript evidence that they were being copied any more ('Breton Lays', 17). The Breton Lay may thus have appeared outmoded to the Franklin's – and to Chaucer's – audience. The imposition of a specific genre may be considered as an attempt on the Franklin's part, as he is revealed to us, to tell the most refined tale he can, under the sting of the Host's remark. He is also attempting to tell a tale which will recommend itself to the *gentil* members of the audience, and which will suggest his own understanding of nobility at the same time (Spearing, 11, 15; Burlin, 60). The choice of Breton Lay, however, suggests a man out of touch with the ways and interests of the nobility, while attempting to ape those ways. The story-pattern of the Tale, so far removed from those of known Breton Lays, suggests real ignorance of the contents of such lays. The tension between the 'given' genre and this apparent realisation of it reveals Chaucer's masterly control of his material whilst at the same time filtering that material through the narrative voice of the character of the Franklin.

Germaine Dempster made clear long ago the implications of the fact that the closest analogue to the *Franklin's Tale* lies in Boccaccio's *Il Filocolo* when she called the claimed Breton origin of the Tale 'one of Chaucer's little impostures' (62). I suggest that the 'little impos-

ture' so evident in the subject-matter of the Tale extends even to its
prologue and the apparent muddled intention of the Teller. The
confusion of ideas about the nature of the Breton lay itself as
expressed in the first seven lines of the Franklin's prologue reinforces the notion that the Franklin is to be seen as far from understanding the nature of this old fashioned aristocratic magical literary genre.

Bibliography

Texts

Chaucer, G., *The Canterbury Tales*, ed. L.D. Benson, Oxford UP,
    Oxford 1988 (all are citations from this edition).
— *The Franklin's Tale*, ed. A.C. Spearing, Cambridge UP, Cambridge
    1966.
Chestre, T., *Sir Launfal*, ed. A.J. Bliss, Nelson's Medieval and
    Renaissance Libr., London 1960.
For *Sir Degaré, Lay le Freine, Emaré, The Erl of Tolous* and *Sir Gowther*
    see T.C. Rumble, ed., *The Breton Lays in Middle English*, Wayne
    State UP, Detroit 1965, repr. 1967.
Gottfried von Strassburg, *Tristan*, ed. R. Bechstein, Deutsche
    Classiker d. Mittelalters 7, 8, Leipzig 1869.
Le Lai de l'Ombre, ed. J. Orr, Edinburgh 1948.
Marie de France, *Lais*, ed. A. Ewert, Blackwell's French Texts,
    Oxford 1944, repr. 1965 (all citations are from this edition).
— *Lais*, ed. K. Warnke, Biblioteca Normannica III, Halle 1885, 3rd
    edn. 1925.
Sir Orfeo, ed. A.J. Bliss, Oxford English Monographs, Oxford 1954,
    rev. 1966 (all citations of Orfeo texts are from this edition, but
    with normalised spellings).
The Romance of Horn, ed. M.K. Pope, *Anglo-Norman Texts 9-10*,
    Oxford 1955, rev. T.B.W. Reid, ANT 12-13, Oxford 1964.
Strandar Strengleikr, in *Strengleikar*, ed. R. Cook and M. Tveitane,
    Oslo 1979, 202-5.
Wace, *Le Roman de Brut*, ed. I.O. Arnold, Societé des Anciens Textes
    Français, Paris 1938-40.

Studies

Beston, J.B., 'How much was known of the Breton *lai* in Fourteenth-
Century England?', in *The Learned and the Lewed* (B.J. Whiting

Festschrift), ed. L.D. Benson, Cambridge Mass. 1974, 319-36.

Bleeth, K., 'The Rocks and the Garden: The Limits of Illusion in Chaucer's *Franklin's Tale*', *English Studies* 74 (1993), 113-23.

Bliss, A.J., '*Sir Orfeo*, Lines 1-46', *English and Germanic Studies* 5 (1952-53), 7-14.

Braswell, M.F., 'The Magic of Machinery: a Context for Chaucer's *Franklin's Tale*', *Mosaic* 18 (1985), 101-10.

Bryan, W.F., and Dempster, G., *Sources and Analogues of Chaucer's Canterbury Tales*, Chaucer Group of the Modern Language Association of America, Chicago 1941, reissued London 1958, 377-97.

Bullock-Davies, C., 'The Form of the Breton Lay', *Medium Aevum* 42 (1973), 18-31.

Burlin, R.B., 'The Art of Chaucer's Franklin', *Neophilologus* 51 (1967), 55-71; also in J.J. Anderson, ed., *Chaucer: The Canterbury Tales*, Macmillan Casebook Series, London 1974, 183-208.

Dempster, G., *Dramatic Irony in Chaucer*, Stanford University Publications, University Series Language and Literature 4.iii, Stanford, California 1932.

Donaldson, E.T., 'Chaucer the Pilgrim', *Publications of the Modern Language Association of America* 69 (1954), 928-36; also in R.J. Schoeck and J. Taylor, eds., *Chaucer Criticism*, U of Notre Dame P, Notre Dame, Indiana 1960-61, I, 1-13.

Donovan, M., *The Breton Lay: A Guide to the Varieties*, U of Notre Dame P, Notre Dame, Indiana and London 1969.

Foulet, L., 'Marie de France et les lais bretons', *Zeitschrift für romanische Philologie* 29 (1905), 19-56 and 293-322.

— 'Le Prologue du *Franklin's Tale* et les lais bretons', *Zeitschrift für romanische Philologie* 30 (1906), 698-711.

Fox, J.C., 'Marie de France', *English Historical Review* 25 (1910), 303-06 and 26 (1911), 317-26.

Gaylord, A.T., 'The Promises in *The Franklin's Tale*', *English Literary History* 31 (1964), 331-65.

Gray, P.E., 'Synthesis and the Double Standard in the *Franklin's Tale*', *Texas Studies in Language and Literature* 7 (1965), 213-24.

Hart, W.M., '*The Franklin's Tale*', in *Haverford Essays: Studies in Honor of F.B. Gummere*, Haverford College, Haverford Pa. 1909, 185-234.

Havely, N.R., *Chaucer's Boccaccio*, Brewer, Woodbridge 1980, 154-61.

Hume, K., 'Why Chaucer calls the *Franklin's Tale* a Breton Lai', *Philological Quarterly* 51 (1972), 365-79.

Johnston, G., 'The Breton Lays in Middle English', in *Iceland and the*

Medieval World (I.R. Maxwell Festschrift), ed. G. Turville-Petre
    and J.S. Martin, Organising Committee for Publishing a Volume
    in Honour of Professor Maxwell, Melbourne 1974, 151-61.
Loomis, L.H., 'Chaucer and the Breton Lays of the Auchinleck MS',
    Studies in Philology 38 (1941), 14-33; also in *Adventures in the
    Middle Ages*, New York 1962, 111-30.
— 'Secular Dramatics in the Royal Palace, Paris 1378, 1389, and
    Chaucer's *Tregetoures*', *Speculum* 33 (1958), 242-55.
Lowes, J.L., 'The *Franklin's Tale*, the *Teseide*, and the *Filocolo*',
    Modern Philology 15 (1917-18), 689-728.
Lucas, A.M., 'Astronomy, Astrology and Magic in Chaucer's
    Franklin's Tale', *The Maynooth Review* 8 (1983), 5-16.
Lucas, P.J., 'The Setting in Brittany of Chaucer's *Franklin's Tale*',
    Poetica 33 (1991), 19-29.
Lucas, P.J. & A.M., 'The Presentation of Marriage and Love in
    Chaucer's *Franklin's Tale*', *English Studies* 72 (1991), 501-12.
Mickel, E.J., 'A Reconsideration of the *Lais* of Marie de France',
    Speculum 46 (1971), 39-65.
Middle English Dictionary, ed. H. Kurath and S.M. Kuhn *et al.*,
    University of Michigan, Ann Arbor 1954-.
Miller, R.P., *Chaucer's Sources*, Oxford UP, New York 1977, 121-35.
Owen Jr., C.A., 'The Crucial Passages in Five of The Canterbury
    Tales: A Study in Irony and Symbol', *Journal of English and
    Germanic Philology* 52 (1953), 294-311; repr. in E. Wagenknecht,
    ed., *Chaucer: Modern Essays in Criticism*, New York 1959.
The Oxford English Dictionary, re-ed. with a Supplement, 13 vols
    (1933); *Supplement*, ed. R.W. Burchfield, 4 vols (1972-86); 2nd
    edn. by J.A. Simpson and E.S.C. Weiner, 20 vols (1980).
Rajna, P., 'Le Origini della novella narrata del Frankleyn nei
    Canterbury Tales del Chaucer', *Romania* 32 (1903), 204-67.
Smithers, G.V., 'Story Patterns in Some Breton Lays', *Medium Aevum*
    22 (1953), 61-92.
Stevens, J., 'The *granz biens* of Marie de France', in *Patterns of Love
    and Courtesy* (memorial volume to C.S. Lewis), ed. J. Lawlor,
    Northwestern UP, Evanston 1966, 1-25.
Tatlock, J.S.P., 'Astrology and Magic in Chaucer's *Franklin's Tale*',
    in *Anniversary Papers for G.L. Kittredge*, New York 1913, 339-50.
— 'The Scene of *The Franklin's Tale* Visited', *Chaucer Society* (ser. 2)
    51, 1914.
Wood, C., *Chaucer and the Country of the Stars*, Princeton N.J., 1970.

Keats and Death
Timor mortis conturbat me (Office of the Dead)

Frank Mc Guinness

I

Control in the poetry of John Keats has always been a matter and a manner of flexibility. The imaginative in his writing depends on the grammatical, for this poetry constructs itself with a strong awareness of its place in a literary universe of fixed degrees, degrees of importance, formal, contextual. At the apex of this universe is one great bright star, and it is to that bright star Keats addresses one of his last sonnets, copied out, predictably, in a blank page of a book containing the works of William Shakespeare.

> Bright Star, would I were stedfast as thou art –
> Not in lone splendor hung aloft the night,
> And watching, with eternal lids apart,
> Like nature's patient, sleepless Eremite,
> The moving waters at their priestlike task
> Of pure ablution round earth's human shores,
> Or gazing on the new soft-fallen masque
> Of snow upon the mountains and the moors –
> No – yet still stedfast, still unchangeable
> Pillow'd upon my fair love's ripening breast,
> To feel for ever its soft swell and fall,
> Awake for ever in a sweet unrest,
> Still, still to hear her tender-taken breath,
> And so live ever – or else swoon to death –

This sonnet's key term is apparently the most neutral but in reality is the most charged. It is 'I', for the remainder of the text concerns itself with a description, a definition of this 'I'. This 'I' is not neutral. Rather it is negative, yet decisively commanding, ordering its identity into being, 'Not' and 'No'. The poem then embodies and disembodies Keats's theory of negative capability, where the poet is everything and nothing, possessing no power so he can assume all powers, going nowhere so he can go everywhere, an empty space waiting to be filled. Voiceless, the poet may speak with many voices, as Keats himself tells us directly in the fragment 'Where's the Poet? Show him! Show him!'

> Where's the Poet? Show him! show him!
> Muses nine, that I may know him!
> 'Tis the man, who with a man
> Is an equal, be he King,
> Or poorest of the beggar-clan,
> Or any other wondrous thing
> A man may be 'twixt ape and Plato;
> 'Tis the man who with a bird,
> Wren or eagle, finds his way to
> All its instincts; – he hath heard
> The Lion's roaring, and can tell
> What his horny throat expresseth;
> And to him the Tiger's yell
> Comes articulate, and presseth
> On his ear like mother-tongue...

This poetry is electric: negative meets positive and produces poetry. It performs, it watches, it cleanses, it revels, it is 'gazing on the new soft-fallen masque/ Of snow upon the mountains and the moors'. Yet the 'I' of Bright Star does not desire such a detached position from which to view human society. He asks for more than sight, he wants touch, 'Still steadfast, still unchangeable/ Pillowed upon my fair love's ripening breast'. There the poet will feel, feel forever, there the poet will awake, and 'awake forever', in a sweet unrest, an unrest like the ecstasy of the Grecian Urn, still, and being still, sweet. From touch of feel and taste of sweet, the poet hears, hears only breath, and it is tender-taken. In this heightened sensuous climax the 'I' divides between the power of the life of the body and the powerlessness, the 'swoon to death'. Poet and poetry divide, the poetry outlasting the poet, for the poem is positive energy, pure energy, the Bright Star, its light identifying the whole earth and its diversity of images, but the poet is a lover, his light is concentrated, shining, illuminating a single figure, 'my fair love', a love that unlike the bright star's looked-on lives, will eventually swoon to death. A conflict, a tension between subject and object emerges, between the nature of poet and poetry, and to connect these separates, there must be action, there must be a verb, and the verb is make, the action of the very making of poetry and poet together. It is a birth and a death, as the ironies of 'La Belle Dame Sans Merci' suggest.

The title comes from a Medieval French poem by Alain Chartier. This alone indicates the landscape of the poem. It belongs to a continent, not a country of poetry. An expanse of territory opens, leaving the reader with a massive sense of distance, yet also a sense of reference. The text is familiar yet remote, familiar in its direct address, remote in its strangeness of subject. Tone and texture vary, and in that variation lies the energy of this meditation on death, not always a *belle dame*, but truly *sans merci*. The lonely knight waits in a blasted environment, soundless, seasonless, although its signs say winter. Disconnected from the surrounding earth, haggard, woe-begone, he lives in a world of sickness, anguish and fever, fading, withering. Illness takes the shape of flowers, lily, rose, a strange association, until the knight speaks of the source of his sickness, 'full beautiful ... a faery's child'. This lady, *la belle dame*, defines her-self in four words, saying 'I love you true.' It is her reward for his intense and abrupt submission to her conquering beauty. The speed of his response to her physical grace carries the language forward like a rapid steed. The gentle harmonies, the clarity of sensual range, create 'sweet moan'. Taste, touch, smell, sound and sight create a 'language strange'. The strange language of love, the love of man and woman. Nourished by desire, love climaxes in consum-mation, happening within 'an elfin grot', where to cease her weep-ing and sighing full sore, he shuts her eyes with kisses, a devouring of the body, and she shuts his eyes with sleep, the sleep of sexual satisfaction but also a paralysis of his body. The power of his sexuality has drained him. This is his last union, his last sleep, his last dream, 'the latest dream'. The elfin grot vanishes, and in its stead there appears a cold hillside, containing the dead of genera-tions past, 'pale kings and princes too, / Pale warriors, death-pale were they all'. The cause of death is not then specified as *la belle dame* herself, but as the sentence under which men place themselves to be in her service. The desperate warnings come too late. The dream dissipates, 'I awoke and found me here,/ On the cold hill's side.' Knocked senseless by physical love, solitary alive in a season-less land, the knight waits on. Waits for what? Perhaps the birds to sing.

> O what can ail thee knight at arms?
> Alone and palely loitering?
> The sedge has withered from the lake
> And no birds sing!

II

Stated in synopsis 'La Belle Dame Sans Merci' emerges as an eerie lament for the loss of male power to female prowess. The barren environment reflects his emasculated state. Vigour gives way to vacuity, and warm-bloodedness to a cold hill's side, packed with pale men who were once alive with political and military import-ance.

Here sleep and dream are sexual conditions, but too strong a sleep, too possessed a dream deprive the sleeping dreamer of fur-ther rest, further activity. The beautiful woman is without mercy because the man has asked for none. She has given as required, say-ing 'I love thee true.' After the gift she weeps and sighs 'full sore', and there receives violence, 'I shut her wild, wild eyes, / With kiss-es four'. And the end of sexual violence is psychic death. Once the master, now the servant, the knight's eyes have grown wild, mad-dened as he is by 'roots of relish sweet', seduced by the pleasures of 'honey wild and manna dew'. In this state he has begun to under-stand a language stranger than love's – the language of death, a language of repetition, or refrain, constant, inescapable, wearying refrain.

> And this is why I sojourne here
> Alone and palely loitering;
> Though the sedge is wither'd from the Lake
> And no birds sing ...

'La Belle Dame Sans Merci' is a poetry of passion, a killer passion, a demon passion, but the demon is human, its magic a meeting of death and love, revealed as the death of love and the love of death. This magic stands at the centre also of 'Ode to a Nightingale'.

III

For the knight of 'La Belle Dame Sans Merci' 'no birds sing.' For the speaker of 'Ode to a Nightingale' all sound seems to aspire to the condition of birdsong. The bird in question, the nightingale, corres-ponds in its beautiful action to the beautiful stillness of the Grecian Urn, 'heard/ In ancient days by emperor and clown'. Through its self-conscious intensity of observable emotion the Grecian Urn purifies our way of seeing: in its unself-conscious intensity of unthinking joy, the Nightingale celebrates our way of hearing. As the Urn engages with the control of our perceptions, the Nightingale instead lies beyond such control, preferring to sing of

itself only to itself, letting the world overhear it by accident, unlike
the design of the Urn. If the 'Ode on a Grecian Urn' is a prayer in
praise of silence and stillness, the 'Ode to a Nightingale' is a burst, a
bolt of melody unleashing the virtues of movement and sound. The
Urn's ecstasy is its static slowness, but the Nightingale dances in its
heartfelt speed. Its poetry is a choreography of light, a medley of
colour and sound, balletic in its grace, frenzied in its stylised operation. The frenzy finds its opposition, its opposition in the poet, as
the opening lines tell us.

> My heart aches, and a drowsy numbness pains
> My sense, as though of hemlock I had drunk,
> Or emptied some dull opiate to the drains
> One minute past, and Lethe-wards had sunk:
> 'Tis not through envy of thy happy lot,
> But being too happy in thine happiness –
> That thou, light-winged Dryad of the trees,
> In some melodious plot
> Of Beechen green, and shadows and numberless,
> Singest of summer in full-throated ease.

This poem of ecstatic physical celebration opens strangely, opens in
a stupor, in drowsy numbness, with a heart aching, suggesting the
poison hemlock carries all before it to the river of death, moving
inexorably Lethe-wards, desiring absolute forgetfulness, the utter
forgetfulness of life itself. As a challenge to this drugged dream,
this infection, comes a 'happy lot', sharing its joy, the nightingale,
'thou light-winged Dryad of the trees'. From the Grecian Urn, 'the
fair youth beneath the trees' now takes wings and shape of a bird,
flitting melodiously through the 'plot'. If in the Grecian Urn 'heard
melodies are sweet, but those unheard are sweeter,' here instead
the heard melody is all. All, because it does more than celebrates its
season, it creates the season, 'summer ... full-throated', at ease in its
method and its medium. But this agent of sound, of melody, this
light bringer, carries with it shadows, 'shadows ... numberless'.
What are they? Who are or who is among their numberless?

> O, for a draught of vintage! that hath been
> Cool'd a long age in the deep-delved earth,
> Tasting of Flora and the country green,
> Dance, and Provençal song, and sunburnt mirth!
> O for a beaker full of the warm South,
> Full of the true, the blushful Hippocrene,
> With beaded bubbles winking at the brim,
> And purple-stained mouth;

> That I might drink, and leave the world unseen,
> And with thee fade away into the forest dim:
>
> Fade far away, dissolve, and quite forget
> What thou among the leaves hast never known,
> The weariness, the fever, and the fret
> Here, where men sit and hear each other groan;
> Where palsy shakes a few, sad, last grey hairs,
> Where youth grows pale, and spectre-thin, and dies;
> Where but to think is to be full of sorrow
> And leaden-eyed despairs,
> Where Beauty cannot keep her lustrous eyes,
> Or new Love pine at them beyond tomorrow.

It is the Nightingale itself, the Nightingale that does not need the drug, the 'draught of vintage', nor the 'beaker full of the warm South'. These belong to time, 'a long age', and to place, 'Provençal ... warm South'. They can be comprehended clearly by the brain, receiving graphic and tactile description. Their material pleasures are lovingly dwelt upon, lovingly imagined, drunk by the nobody poet so that the somebody Keats can dissolve into sweet oblivion, the oblivion of the 'world unseen', the world unseen that in its sweetness turns into the Nightingale's abode, the abode of the 'forest dim'; this forest is a place to 'fade away', but the fading is for the poet, not the Nightingale. Unseen, it may be heard: unheard, he cannot be seen. For what is there to see, what is there to hear? 'What thou among the leaves have never known.' That is the pain of weariness, fever, fret, caught in the single swoon of 'groan'. The dying man catches a glimpse of his own corpse already manifesting itself in his decaying body, palsied, grey, pale, spectre-thin, betrayed by its physical mortality. The freedom of flight that is the Nightingale's contrasts with the earthbound burden of the human body, but not for long. If flesh in its full heaviness cannot rise, the voice still can and take the eyes with it.

> Away! away! for I will fly to thee,
> Not charioted by Bacchus and his pards,
> But on the viewless wings of Poesy,
> Though the dull brain perplexes and retards:
> Already with thee! tender is the night,
> And haply the Queen-Moon is on her throne,
> Cluster'd around by all her starry Fays;
> But here there is no light,
> Save what from heaven is with the breezes blown
> Through verdurous glooms and winding mossy ways.

The voice here acts as agent of air, a vehicle to transcend earth, carrying with it 'on the viewless wings of Poesy' the disruptive ecstasy of its own uplifting power to defy expectations, to confront conventions, not least those of the poem's preceding stanzas. After the gloom, we hear 'tender is the night.' The moon is happy, the hemlock spilt and forgotten, because it is not the god of wine, 'Bacchus', nor his pards that have created this visionary voice. It is enlivened by 'no light' save that which is heavensent. In this divine, stable ecstasy, what is to be seen?

> I cannot see what flowers are at my feet,
> Nor what soft incense hangs upon the boughs,
> But, in embalmed darkness, guess each sweet
> Wherewith the seasonable month endows
> The grass, the thicket, and the fruit-tree wild;
> White hawthorn, and the pastoral eglantine;
> Fast fading violets cover'd up in leaves;
> And mid-May's eldest child,
> The coming musk-rose, full of dewy wine,
> The murmurous haunt of flies on summer eves.

All this the body experiences, the body knows. It is still free to abandon itself to the sources of pleasure. They are natural, grass, thicket, fruit-tree wild, hawthorn, pastoral eglantine, fast fading violets, coming musk rose. But in the midst of these silent, scented sights come sounds, the ominous pun on haunt, 'the murmurous haunt of flies on summer eves,' drunk like the speaker earlier in the poem, this time with 'dewy wine', but wine nonetheless, a wine of 'dull opiate', bringing with it drunkenness, the drunkenness of death.

> Darkling I listen; and, for many a time
> I have been half in love with easeful Death,
> Call'd him soft names in many a mused rhyme,
> To take into the air my quiet breath;
> Now more than ever seems it rich to die,
> To cease upon the midnight with no pain,
> While thou art pouring forth thy soul abroad
> In such an ecstasy!
> Still wouldst thou sing, and I have ears in vain –
> To thy high requiem become a sod.

In such a state dying begins, the sensuous decay of the body. And death is embraced as lover, masterful lover, requiring submission to his masculine command. The poetry is passive, teased into play by the power of death, energised by the Nightingale, 'pouring forth

thy soul abroad / In such an ecstasy'. This energy will invigorate
but also outlast the receptive, feeling body of the poet, 'Still wouldst
thou sing, and I have ears in vain - / To thy high requiem become a
sod.' The bed, the grave of the earth, is where this relationship will
be finally consummated, but love of death and death of love are
already partners, linking as they do the subject of feeler and the
object of feeling. The soft name-calling of dying man for lover death
continues.

> Thou wast not born for death, immortal Bird!
> No hungry generations tread thee down;
> The voice I hear this passing night was heard
> In ancient days by emperor and clown:
> Perhaps the self-same song that found a path
> Through the sad heart of Ruth, when, sick for home,
> She stood in tears amid the alien corn;
> The same that oft-times hath
> Charm'd magic casements, opening on the foam
> Of perilous seas, in faery lands forlorn.

From the intense psychology of an interior history in the last stanza,
now there is concentration on ancient histories, Roman and Jewish.
A passing night, a sad heart, the sickness for home, all contrast with
the 'immortal Bird' with its immortal song. Its music is unchanging,
a radical opposition to the teeming shifts of imagery that separate
the 'hungry generations'. Being hungry, they will devour the 'alien
corn', earning their bread of life 'in tears', isolated from 'the voice'
heard this passing night. Its sense of eternity differs utterly from the
changes of human experience, the diversity of cultures, from
'emperor and clown' of Rome to the Moabite Ruth, herself a traveller to Bethlehem, to an alien land. A promised land. But that land
is foreign, is exile, and is not a 'faery land'. It is similar to the land of
'charm'd magic casements' in only one, vital respect. They are both
'forlorn'. Why?

> Forlorn! the very word is like a bell
> To toll me back from thee to my sole self!
> Adieu! the fancy cannot cheat so well
> As she is fam'd to do, deceiving elf.
> Adieu! adieu! thy plaintive anthem fades
> Past the near meadows, over the still stream,
> Up the hill-side; and now 'tis buried deep
> In the next valley-glades:
> Was it a vision, or a waking dream?
> Fled is that music: – Do I wake or sleep?

They are both forlorn because both are the creation of what Keats pinpoints as the poet's 'sole self', a self that rings like a warning bell, 'a bell / to toll me back', back from make believe, from the world of pretend, above all back from the world of the 'immortal Bird'. Its plaintive anthem fades, and with that fading goes the certainty, the clarity and the verbal assuredness of the vision. The physical doubt of distance emerges, and that physical doubt gives way to psychic doubt, 'Was it a vision, or a waking dream?' That question, unanswered, leads to another unanswered question, 'Do I wake or sleep?' The urging is to wake, for reality has intruded in the form of observation, 'Fled is that music.' Leaving what behind? A memory, a music of revelation, a fear of death, a love of fear. 'Ode to a Nightingale' is at once a *memento mori* and a dance of death, a brilliant Keatsian contradiction, a creature of earth and air, of shoe and wonder, as he anticipated it would be in the closing lines of his 'song about myself', 'There was a Naughty Boy':

So he stood in
His shoes
And he wondered
He wondered
He stood in his
Shoes and he wonder'd ...

Bibliography

Keats, John, *Poems*, Oxford Poetry Library, ed. Elizabeth Cook, Oxford UP, Oxford/New York 1994.

'The Night Side of Nature':

Henry Ferris, Writing the Dark Gods of Silence

Richard Hayes

I

The Wellesley Index to Victorian Periodicals assigns thirty articles in *The Dublin University Magazine* to Henry Ferris for the period 1839 to 1851 (Houghton). Writing where so little has been written before, how does one begin to examine these texts left to us? A consideration of the evidence the *Wellesley Index* provides for the attribution of these articles to Ferris might serve as one place to begin. Attributions are based on a thin set of textual traces: the anagrammatic name 'Irys Herfner' when deciphered reads 'Henry Ferris', the name 'Ferris' appears opposite a small number of articles in the Charles Lever records for Lever's period as editor of the *DUM*, and an entry in a catalogue of Trinity College Dublin students records Ferris' presence in the college in the early 1800s. A web of textual comparison and cross-reference helps attribute articles for which such external evidence does not exist. Out of these traces the canon of texts attributed to Ferris is constructed, and out of these traces a biography of Ferris might be written. One might begin here. However on closer examination much of this evidence is seen to be unsatisfactory, and often quite dubious, especially that evidence based on 'internal' resemblances in style, setting, and subject-matter.[1] Moreover the very relevance of seeking attributions like this may be called into question. As a reader of the *DUM* one encounters these texts without the collage of evidence that posits an originary moment in an author Henry Ferris – not one of the texts is ever signed in that name, and, consistent with the *DUM*'s general policy, most of the texts attributed to Ferris are not signed at all. I would like to begin here, as a reader. Doing so entails abandoning an assigning (as/sign/ing), attributing role, and beginning by reading not texts by Ferris but what I would like to call the Ferris-texts. These Ferris-texts do not exist in isolation, but rather take place in and, I would like to argue, are expressive of, a larger context (con/text). A reading then of the Ferris-texts involves also a reading

of the contexts into which they fit. The aim of this essay is to read
and examine the Ferris-texts by way of, and in terms of, an examination of the relationship between the Ferris-texts and their larger
context.

II

Into what contexts can we place the Ferris-texts? The immediate
context into which they fit is of course the *DUM*. To the reader, the
very fact of the appearance of these texts in the *DUM* aligns them
with certain social, political, cultural and religious positions – every
article in the magazine can be seen to be countersigned by a larger
unified and unifying voice, perhaps that of the phantom figure of
'Anthony Poplar', expressive of an often quite partisan advocacy of
Tory, Unionist and sectarian Protestant interests. Before proceeding
to consider the Ferris-texts in the context of the *DUM*, however, a
second, perhaps more fundamental context must be elucidated.
This context may best be introduced by means of the word 'occult' –
with articles like 'Miscellanea Mystica', 'An Evening with the
Witchfinders', and 'Night in a Haunted House', one may, in the
most general sense, describe the Ferris-texts as texts concerned with
the 'occult'. What is meant by this word? According to the Oxford
English Dictionary a primary meaning of the word is simply 'hidden' or 'concealed'. Proceeding further, however, an interesting
duality in the word can be exposed. 'Occult' can refer on the one
hand to that which is 'Not apprehended, or not apprehensible, by
the mind; beyond the range of understanding or of ordinary knowledge; recondite; mysterious.' This perhaps accords with the usual
usage of the word to refer to something vaguely supernatural. A
second meaning, however, proposes that 'occult' was 'Applied in
early science or natural philosophy to physical qualities not manifest to direct observation but discoverable only by experiment, or to
those whose nature was unknown or unexplained; latent.' At once
then 'occult' is associated with (a) the hidden as inaccessibly hidden, and with (b) the hidden as discoverable by experiment.

We may extend this second application of the word further by
associating it with one particular interest of the Ferris-texts. The
vast majority of the Ferris-texts are in some way concerned with
what is called 'occult science', a term that specifies at once both an
object and (significantly) a mode of inquiry. The object of the
inquiries of many of the Ferris-texts is the 'occult sciences', ancient
pseudo-sciences 'held to involve the knowledge or use of agencies

of a secret and mysterious nature' (*OED*). Among these occult sciences one may include theosophy, astrology and, the obsession it seems of the Ferris-texts, mesmerism. 'Occult science' also however refers to a mode of inquiry, a 'scientific' approach to the occult, to revealing what is hidden. We may then place the Ferris-texts in a second context, that of nineteenth-century science.

A detailed elucidation of what 'science' and 'scientific' means in the nineteenth-century is beyond the scope of this essay. One may, however, point briefly to a number of key characteristics of science for that period. Alexander Pope's epitaph for Isaac Newton, though written in 1735, provides a useful introduction:

> Nature and Nature's Laws lay hid in Night:
> God said, Let Newton be! and all was Light.
>
> (Pope, 92)

Firstly, science in the nineteenth century, embodied for many in the figure of Newton, fundamentally meant empirical science. Though the word 'empirical' causes some problems of definition, one may say that empirical science is science based on experiment rather than on abstract thought (Flew, 97). In turn the word 'experiment' proves complicated. 'Experiment' is closely tied to the word 'experience', which may refer to experiences of either an internal/inner or an external/outer kind. Crucial for our discussion here is the alignment of empirical science and experiment with the outer/external realm of experience (Williams, 278). Empirical science, the science of the nineteenth-century, becomes then the science of the external world, of 'Nature and Nature's Laws'.

A fundamental aspect of the notion of 'experiment' is its verifiability and the concomitant association of empirical/experimental science with objectivity. In a crucial sense empirical science in the nineteenth century became the test of objectivity (Williams, 278). In other words, a second characteristic of science in the nineteenth century is that empirical science in the nineteenth century came to be taken as the norm of truth. In an important extension of this, Walter Cannon argues that not only was empirical science the norm of truth but that it also provided the only available language in which truth could be expressed (Cannon, 487-502). The theologian Edward Pusey, for example, in an attempt to refute science, argues that 'All the sciences move like planets around the sun of God's truth', thus using the language of astronomy, of science, the very language of that which he seeks to refute (see Cannon, 498).

Pusey's attempt to refute science brings us neatly to a consideration of a third aspect of science in the nineteenth century, namely its application to religious belief. As early as 1674 Robert Boyle applied what he called the 'mechanical philosophy' to a universe ruled by God, and concluded that 'God gave motion to matter', 'established those rules of motion and that order amongst things corporeal, which we are wont to call the laws of nature' and, 'upheld by his incessant concourse and general providence', the phenomena of the universe proceed 'according to mechanical laws' (Boyle, 138-39). Boyle can be seen as providing a similar conclusion to that of William Paley's infamous 'design argument' for the existence of God, which appeared in his 1802 publication *Natural Theology, or Evidence of the Existence and Attributes of the Deity collected from the Appearances of Nature*, the title of which illustrates well Paley's mode of procedure. Given the existence of designed and orderly mechanical contrivances (Paley takes the example of a watch) and thus the necessary existence of designers for these objects (the watchmaker), one may proceed by analogy to show that since similar order and design exists in the natural world, there must necessarily exist a Designer God, a Divine Watchmaker (Hick, 99-103). This argument from design proved a popular argument for God's existence certainly throughout the early part of the nineteenth-century.

Paley however can be seen as entering this 'design' debate rather late. The argument had already been formulated by, amongst others, Cicero and Thomas Aquinas, and was devastatingly criticised by David Hume and other Deists in the eighteenth-century. Hans Eichner points to the unacceptable implications of Boyle's 'mechanical philosophy' for the religious believer, implications that are equally applicable to the argument from design. The watch, once set in motion, has no further need for a designer – God then can be seen as a being who has abandoned the cosmos to its own devices, as a being who never interferes in the mechanism he has created, and in fact, by the perfection of his creation, as a being who has rendered such interference unnecessary. Secondly, the Divine Designer's mechanism neither grows nor develops – presumably as an all perfect being this Designer created the best possible world. Thus progress towards a better world is illusory, and thus, by implication, the existence of evil in the world would seem to be necessary to it. Thirdly the view that sees the living natural world as a vast mechanism seems to prompt the view that all living beings are like machines. Consciousness then becomes a 'ghost in the machine', and ultimately one is forced to conclude that free-will cannot and does not exist (Eichner, 10-12). In this universe, a vast machine closed to all external influence, governed by its own internal laws, man plays a tiny, determined role.

This movement of applying the 'mechanical philosophy' to the cosmos thus involves a reduction of God's role in the universe, ultimately culminating in a total removal of God from nature. At this point we can refer back to the idea that there are two spheres of human experience: inner/internal experience and outer/external experience. We have seen that it is the outer/external world that is the domain of empirical/experimental science. Coincident with the removal of God from nature and the external world, we find that the inner realm becomes associated more and more with religion, as well as with art, imagination, and the irrational (Williams, 278). Experience in this inner realm was subjective, the scientist would argue, as it was experimentally unverifiable. Thus inner experience, the realm of the gods, became at best a realm above truth (supernatural), but more often a realm that could be counted false and illusory.

This led Thomas Carlyle, in his essay 'Signs of the Times' (1829), to denounce what he saw as 'the Mechanical Age', an age devoted totally to the external (Carlyle, 99-118). Significantly for Carlyle the mechanical rule extended into every walk of life: 'It is the Age of the Machine,' he writes, 'in every outward and inward sense of the word' (Carlyle, 100). For Carlyle the 'intellectual bias' of the day proposed that 'except the external, there are no true sciences', and

> that to the inward world (if there be any) our only conceivable road is through the outward; that, in short, what cannot be investigated and understood mechanically, cannot be investigated and understood at all. (Carlyle, 105)

This statement is echoed in the Ferris-texts when in 'German Ghosts and Ghost-seers (I)' it is suggested that it is the boast of the nineteenth-century that it gives itself

> wholly to those studies in which sense and the sensuous understanding are at home, accounting the extra-sensuous synonymous with the visionary – yea, the non-sensible equivalent to the nonsensical. (33)[2]

It is important to emphasise the pervasiveness of this devotion to the external in nineteenth-century society. The age was mechanical in its economic and political philosophies, as well as in its science. The utilitarian philosophies of Bentham and Mill encouraged new, 'man-centred', secular policies, judging the good in proportion as it produced the happiness of the greater number of people. The application of this norm of utility, and in general of scientific principles,

to the sphere of government culminated in the rise of the state-cen-
tred economy, guided by principles of expediency and efficiency.
Ultimately the rise of this 'scientific state' signals, in a fundamental
sense, a transfer of power from God to man, where value and truth
reside in the external world, and religion becomes the preserve of
the internal, the private and personal concern of the individual citizen. One could suggest at this point that the Ferris-texts, with their
general interest in the 'occult' and 'occult' phenomena, are expressive of a reaction against the temper of this age and its rejection of
the internal, and are an attempt to re-assert the authenticity of the
internal as a realm of experience.

In what sense can the Ferris-texts be seen as such a reaction? It is
important here to remind ourselves of the crucial duality of meaning in the word 'occult' alluded to earlier on. As we have seen,
'occult' refers to two senses in which something can be hidden: it
can refer to that which is hidden and cannot be revealed, and also to
that which is hidden but revealable by experiment. In this second
sense, the 'occult' can be considered accessible to experimental science, to the nineteenth-century science of the external. Do the
Ferris-texts refer to the 'occult' in this sense of the word? To do so
would surely be merely to extend the realm of the mechanical further, denying the authenticity and existence of a supernatural,
internal world. It is clear, however, from a number of the Ferris-
texts, that the 'occult' here means more than this. In 'Of the
Nightmare' it is proposed that two realms exist:

> Everything has its transcendental or supersensuous side, as well
> as its phenomenal side; and science has to do wholly with the
> latter ... while faith, imagination, instinctive intuition, which is
> strongest in the unscientific man, goes direct to the unknown,
> inaccessible substance. (38)

Significantly it is only to the 'unscientific mind' that the supersensuous
world is available. Recalling Pope's equation of Newton with the
bringing of light to the darkness in the epitaph quoted earlier, the
existence of an internal world beyond science is further asserted in
a crucial passage in 'Miscellanea Mystica (I)':

> he that will know nothing of mysticism – he that will be always
> consequent, always logical, always clear-sighted and wide
> awake – is shut up to a very narrow view of himself and all
> around him. If it were always day, the remoter regions of creat-
> ion would remain for ever unknown to us ... Sense, and its kind-
> red power of understanding, while they subject to our cogni-

sance the whole sphere of the material, the external, so shut up the inward organs of the soul, that we know not so much as that there is a sphere of the spiritual ... there are worlds, within and without us, which can be seen only by their own light, which all other light eclipses. No one sees so little as he whose eyes are always open. (177)

The 'occult' then in the Ferris-texts refers not to a scientifically accessible world, but to an internal, supernatural world, beyond the reach of the light of science.

However, following from this equation of the occult with that which is beyond science, a crucial paradox in the project of the Ferris-texts is exposed. The concern of the texts is to argue for, or more precisely, perhaps, to prove the existence of the supernatural world to an unbelieving and mechanical nineteenth century. At the same time what the texts wish to prove lies beyond proof – the supernatural world lies beyond scientific inquiry, the mode of proof (and truth) for the mechanical age. 'Occult science' is then a paradoxical enterprise, for it cannot scientifically approach what is, by definition, beyond science. In the passage from 'Miscellanea Mystica' quoted above, it is suggested that light (to be equated, as we have seen, with science) can only encompass a certain amount of human experience, and that there exists a realm of darkness beyond it, to which it cannot reach. This darkness we may refer to as the 'night side of nature' (alluding to a book mentioned in 'A Night in the Bell Inn': see Crowe), a side accessible not to that which enlightens as to nature's laws, but only to the unscientific mind. The project of the Ferris-texts must then be seen as in some measure anti-scientific – its aim is to prove the failure of science to penetrate totally the darkness. In this it must also, paradoxically, frustrate and disrupt itself.

To examine this paradox more closely, we must consider how the Ferris-texts proceed with the action of 'proving'. What sort of 'proof' is offered? Many of the texts proceed by citing 'cases' and speculating 'scientifically' about them. In 'Mare's Nests', for example, selected cases are given – the case of Fra Vito, the levitating Calabrian monk, for instance – and various explanatory theories expounded about them, most proceeding towards an explanation of the phenomena based on mesmerism and magnetism. Similarly, in the three lengthy articles on mesmerism, perhaps the most apparently 'scientific' of the Ferris-texts, theories of the magnet are propounded and cases of healing by magnets, of mesmeric sleep and magnetic clairvoyance are presented as evidence.[3] However we have seen that truth in the nineteenth-century demanded verifiable, experimental evidence – the Ferris-texts cannot meet that demand. What is offered by the Ferris-texts is not sound, empirically verifiable evidence, but a series of subjective cases, stories, anecdotes, unverifiable, unrepeatable, unscientific, and ultimately unsatisfactory as far as the Mechanical Age is concerned. This difficulty with providing evidence for occult phenomena like mesmerism is symptomatic of the degree to which the occult realm the Ferris-texts are concerned with lies beyond the confines of experimental science, and is open only to 'unscientific' procedure. However the nature of the evidence that is provided – the subjective story – points to a crucial distinction made frequently in the Ferris-texts which may help in elucidating further the paradox of their project. That distinction is between 'narrative' and 'theory'.

Two passages stand out as significant. In 'A Pilgrimage to Caldaro', an account of a visit to an 'estatica' in Italy, the narrator begins to 'theorise', and speculates that what he has seen is an excellent example of mesmeric clairvoyance. The girl presents a clear example of 'spontaneous clairvoyance', we are told, a 'higher order' of clairvoyance than those 'artificially produced' by any mesmerist. Then, in a statement which might echo through all the Ferris-texts, we are told that 'my business here is rather to narrate than to theorise' (312). What 'theory' means in the Ferris-texts is made clear in a passage from 'Mesmerism (II)' where we are told that

> the time is not yet ripe for a theory of Mesmerism that will stand … Nevertheless theorizing is a spontaneous operation of the mind … While we are observing facts, our theory is silently forming itself; for what else, indeed, is a theory but a beholding? My theory of the Mesmeric phenomena is … what *I see* in the Mesmeric phenomena. Not to theorize is not to look, but passively suffer the shapes of things to flit over the incognizant sense … let us theorise … as we go on … The very terminology of our record will depend in some measure on the theory – on the light in which, on the medium through which we see. (287)

The reappearance of the dark/light metaphor here is significant. In equating 'theory' with seeing (bearing in mind the 'Miscellanea Mystica' passage quoted earlier) and with light ('theory' is 'the light in which … the medium through which we see'), 'theory' is aligned closely with experimental science, the light of which the Ferris-texts are determined to show is of limited strength. 'Theory' can thus be seen as an inadequate mode for referring to the occult.

'Narrative', however, does provide an adequate mode of reference. 'Narrative', in many ways, can be equated with the verb 'to display': 'to depict, describe, exhibit, to set forth at large, expound; to unfold (a tale)' (*OED*). In referring to the supernatural, 'theory' is inadequate – one is forced to display the truth of the supernatural rather than prove it. In the Ferris-texts this display takes the form of 'cases' – tales, stories, narratives – which are unfolded as evidence for the existence of the internal, supernatural world. The paradox of the project of the Ferris-texts is then their attempt to 'theorise' about that which can by definition only be 'narrated'.

The 'theory'/'narrative' dichotomy can however be pushed a stage further. In 'A Pilgrimage to Caldaro', in the paragraph immediately following the declaration of a determination to narrate rather than theorise mentioned earlier, we find a long, quite dramatic description of Maria Mörl, the girl whom the narrator has come to visit. One can note initially that the leap from rather cold to dramatic prose signals the leap from the 'theoretical' to the 'narrative' mode. More significantly in this dramatic descriptive paragraph, however, is the self-confessed failure of the description to fully convey the experience. The girl, we are told,

> impressed me, I will confess, as I stood there, alone in her presence, with feelings which I have not words to convey. (312)

This failure of words to convey the experience perhaps hints at a meaning of 'narrative' beyond merely displaying the truth in a story. 'Narrative' may be extended in meaning to signify (*sign*/ify?), in some way, the actual experience itself, the experience of the supernatural which, as we have seen, is *beyond words*. Words on the page then may be seen to fall on the 'theoretical' side of the divide, so that '*theory*/*science*/*text* can be aligned, and can be seen to refer to the external/natural world, while '*narrative*'/*the unscientific*/— refers to the internal/supernatural world.

In this sense then the 'cases' that are cited in the Ferris-texts are frustrated attempts to display an experience. Words on the page exist and are permanent in the external world, are the vehicle of science, of light, are the expressions of theory. The experience of the supernatural by necessity is beyond all these things. The paradox of the Ferris-texts then becomes an attempt to objectively convey what is a subjective experience, to re-create on the bright, white page the experience of the night side of nature.

III

Into this larger epistemic context a smaller, more immediate context (con/*text*) for the Ferris-texts is inscribed (in/*scribe*/d), that of the *DUM*. I have already mentioned that the *DUM* can be seen as the firm advocate of Tory, Unionist Protestantism in early-/mid-nineteenth-century Ireland. In the following consideration of the relationship between the Ferris-texts and the *DUM*, I would like to concentrate on the Protestantism of the magazine. It is true to say that, if anything, the *DUM* was the voice of the Established Church in Ireland. We may begin our inquiry then by examining the state of the Established Church during the period covered by the Ferris-texts.

Without doubt this period was a time of rapid and radical change for the Church, change which was initiated by the influence of the so-called 'New Reformation', an injection of a new spirit of evangelicism into the Church from the 1820s on. The idea that a new 'spirit' was introduced into the Church is significant. Fundamentally the 'New Reformation' can be characterised as a reaction against the too rigid application of science and reason to matters of religion, a response that echoes, and is echoed by, the responses to the Mechanical Age by Carlyle and the Ferris-texts. The new spirit in the Established Church can thus be seen as a reaction to the ending of God's reign initiated by the influence of the mechanical philosophy, a reaction that sought to restore God to his place as originary creator and sustainer of the cosmos. The new spirit was carried perhaps too far for the Established Church, by groups like the Irvingites or, more famously, the Oxford Movement, all of whom were seen to abandon the 'critical faculty' (Drummond, 155). While stressing the importance of a new 'spirit', the Church never sought to abandon reason totally, but merely to limit its application. The 'New Reformation' determined that `internal religion' be placed above `external ordinances' (Emerson, 331), thus making a similar distinction to that made by the Ferris-texts, stressing the internal, unscientific world at the expense of the world outside, the only realm to which science and reason have application.

The immersion of the Established Church in this new evangelical spirit finds two connected expressions outside the Church in the foundation of the Bible Society, with a concomitant renewal of emphasis on Scripture, and in a renewed proselytising effort to the Irish Catholics (Brynn, 411-12). These two movements are intimately

connected, for the missionary impulse – expressed in groups like
the Society for Irish Church Missions to the Roman Catholics,
founded by A.C. Dallas – was founded in Scripture and, most
importantly, was conducted *by means of* Scripture. The profession of
'truth' was essential to the whole project of the missionary – one
had first to be seen to proclaim the 'truth', then one could proceed
to bring people to a greater knowledge of it. It was in Scripture that
truth was to be found for the Protestant evangelist. However 'truth'
resides in Scripture (*script*/ure) for a more fundamental reason than
the proclaimed veracity of its dictates and doctrines. Rather
Scripture is true, in a fundamental sense in the nineteenth-century,
because it exists in printed form.

A trust in the truth of the printed word is expressed in the means
by which the Protestant evangelist proceeded with the process of
converting. One may point initially to the deluge of polemical pam-
phlets and printed sermons that appeared in the period between
1822 and 1869. The printed sermon, in fact, became the principal
weapon of the Protestant proselytiser (*prose*/lytiser) in a pamphlet
war that characterised Protestant-Catholic relations in this period
(Bowen, 88-89). Moreover the Bible was translated and printed in
the Irish language, and became instrumental in the process of
bringing 'truth' to the Catholics of the West of Ireland. The most
famous and influential of Protestant missionaries, the aforemen-
tioned A.C. Dallas, also staked his claim with the printed page – his
A Voice from Heaven to Ireland was published in 1846. Utilising to the
full the advances of technology in the printing trade, Dallas' tract
was mass-produced and 20,000 copies were circulated among
Roman Catholics, each copy arriving by penny post on 16 January
1846.[4] This willingness to utilise the technology of the Mechanical
Age, to put things into print, and thus to place a trust in the printed
word as embodying truth, serves to align the evangelical Protestant
firmly with the science of the nineteenth-century, the truths of
which were also, as we have seen, embodied and expressed in the
printed word.

This alignment of the evangelist with science perhaps suggests a
conflict of commitments that reflects the epistemic paradox of the
Ferris-texts elucidated earlier. The fundamental impulse behind the
project of the evangelical movement was a reassertion of the validity
and importance of the spiritual, the inward, the occult, the unscientific. At the same time this impulse expresses itself, within the proselytising effort towards Catholics, in a belief in the truths of science
in the form of a commitment to the printed word as embodying

truth. Thus one evangelical Protestant could say:

> It is my duty to attend to the Scriptures, and to place nothing on
> a level with them which comes, as far as I can judge, from mere
> ordinary human beings (Anon., *Conversation*, 4),

and at the same time, with other ordinary human beings, mechani-
cally print and mass-produce those Scriptures. At the root of the
problem is the conflict that mirrors, and is mirrored by, the Ferris-
texts. Both are forced to adopt a scientific mode (the printed word),
the only mode that is accepted as true, to promulgate a message
that is quite outside the bounds of that mode (the supernatural – by
definition inaccessible to, and inexpressible in, the printed word, in
scripture). A question we might pose, and leave for the moment
unanswered, is whether this conflict in the evangelical project is
expressive of a deeper, more pervasive epistemic crisis also
expressed in the Ferris-texts, or whether the conflict in the Ferris-
texts, if it reflects anything at all, simply reflects in the *DUM* this
conflict in the evangelical project, without reference to any deeper
disruption.

I mentioned earlier that the Protestant-Catholic struggle was
played out, to a great degree, in a large-scale pamphlet war. The
Protestant response to the printed matter emanating from the
Catholic side is interesting, and casts some light on their own position. In *A Voice from Heaven to Ireland*, A.C. Dallas argues that the
Catholics of Ireland suffer under a tyrannical 'Italian ruler', a ruler
who 'put the yoke upon the neck, under the warrant of the book of
which he showed but the outside' (Dallas, 197). Significantly the
Catholic does not encounter the printed word (wherein lies the
'truth') but is rather shown only the outside of the book. The content of the Catholic book, when and if revealed, one writer argues,
is,

> a demi-Christian mythology, which bears but a very indistinct
> resemblance to the story of the Bible – a mass of fiction, founded
> ... on the scriptural narrative, but utterly and entirely unlike it.
> (Anon., *Roman Catholic Devotion*, 284)

Catholic print is then denounced as 'untrue' – not only is it totally
unlike Scripture, but, as it is often only the cover of the book that is
revealed, it cannot be counted in many ways as printed matter at
all. Given also the identification of the Catholic print with 'myth',
and myth's association with 'fable'/'fabulous' (Williams, 211), an
interesting conclusion may be arrived at. Here the Catholic is
aligned, most firmly, with occult/supernatural/inward, with 'nar-

rative', and, in opposition to this, the Protestant, despite his evangelical leanings, is associated with science/nature/outward, with 'theory'.

This occult/Catholic conjunction is frequently made, often more overtly, in Protestant texts of this period. In 'A Pilgrimage to Caldaro', one of the Ferris-texts referred to earlier, the journey to Italy, the seat of Roman Catholicism, is prefaced with remarks by the narrator equating travelling with dreaming (307), thus in some way associating Italy with the land of the dream, and Catholicism with the inward/occult realm. Such associations are made throughout the Ferris-texts.[5] More overtly, the full title of Mortimer O'Sullivan and R.J. McGhee's *Romanism as it Rules in Ireland* specifies this occult/Catholic relationship, and further reminds us of the crucial sense in which occult means 'hidden': *Romanism as it Rules in Ireland: being a full and authentic report of the meetings held in various parts of England and Scotland, in which the theology secretly taught, the commentary on the Bible clandestinely circulated, the law of the Papal States surreptitiously set up to govern Ireland, and the Secret Diocesan Statutes of the Province of Leinster, have been successively detected and exposed, together with all the important documents relating to the subject, selected and arranged with a copious index* (O'Sullivan and McGhee). The sense in which the authors (evangelical Protestants) 'expose', 'detect' and 'index' the secrets of the Catholic leads us to associate the Protestant with the scientist, bringing light to the darkness of Catholicism, revealing all that dwells in that night.

A further examination of the alignment posited between 'occult' and 'Catholic' yields some interesting conclusions that provide insight into many of the concerns of the Ferris-texts. We may begin to elucidate this link by examining the way in which the Catholic is represented in Protestant texts. Two key representations abound. Firstly, the Catholic is accounted an emotional being, and as such is irrational, lacking in judgement and reasonableness. Recalling the sense in which, for the Mechanical Age, the inward became the realm of the irrational and emotional, as well as of the occult, the significance of this representation is obvious. A second common representation, however, suggests a cause for this lack of reason. The Catholic is seen as being held a slave by the priest to whom he has surrendered his reason in the shape of his conscience (con/*science*), his faculty for judgement. The confessional, target of many of the most vicious of Protestant attacks, became the site of this surrender, the place where, in darkness, the Catholic conscience is externalised and given over to the priest. (Interestingly, in a further link between Catholicism and the occult, ghosts are presented in 'German Ghosts and Ghost-seers (II)' as the 'spectral birth of the imagination ... fecundated by conscience' (225), in many ways presenting the ghost as conscience externalised.) The moment of surrender of the conscience hurls the Catholic back on his emotions, places him at the mercy of the priest, and, in a fundamental way, empties him of human identity and personhood.[6] The individual thus becomes victim of a system larger than himself, and becomes an automaton devoid of identity within 'an infernal machine, plied by the Satanic sons of Loyola' (O'Beirne, 16).

The Protestant, in contrast, retains his conscience (con/*science*) and thus his identity as an individual. 'Liberty of conscience' was frequently stressed by Protestant writers as a fundamental tenet of their faith, a faith that sought always to ensure the protection and validity of the individual. Thus 'liberty of conscience' is

> that principle which secures to man that liberty which is the birth-right of a rational and immortal being, and makes him an accountable being, not to his fellow-creatures, but to his God.
>
> (O'Sullivan and McGhee, 608)

The 'engine' of Catholicism, stealing from the individual believer this fundamental human principle, thus places itself in direct opposition to Protestantism, seeking to undermine, as it does, the very basis of the Protestant faith. However the association of Catholicism with machinery reflects a second system also guilty of undermining Protestant individuality. This second oppressive system was the 'scientific state' we spoke of earlier, which was at the time taking firm hold in the Union. The effect of new policies from London, based on utilitarian, scientific principles of efficiency and expediency, was one which discriminated against the Irish Protestant especially, in many ways reducing him to a second-class citizen of the Union. Efficiency determined that state institutions be centralised and that the population be integrated – thus subgroups, like the Irish Protestant, were pushed to the margins of influence and power. Here officialdom was experienced as alien and impersonal, and as destructive of the individual (see Hill). Thus the Board of Education, one arm of the 'scientific state' felt by the Irish Protestant, became also an 'engine', and was significantly seen by one writer as 'a vast machinery for the administration of the strongest preparation of Popery' (Anon., 'A New Batch of Saints', 717).

Catholicism and the 'scientific state' became in many ways analogous, both seen as oppressive of the individual. Caught between these two impersonal systems, the Protestant had to assert, in the strongest possible sense, his own identity, his validity as an individual. The defence of the validity of the inward/occult by texts like the Ferris-texts then takes on additional significance, placing, as it does, the subjective individual experience in opposition to overwhelming forces massed against it. Occult texts then become expressive in some way of this attempt to assert the importance of the individual's identity. This position is refracted in *The Zoist*, a magazine devoted to the legitimation of mesmerism and phrenology as sciences, which frequently sees itself as 'a small knot of natural philosophers' who are victims of a larger 'religious crusade' (Anon., 'The Christian Remembrancer', or 'Arrogance Unmasked', 314).[7] At the same time the Irish Protestant evangelists could claim to be 'a small knot of religious believers', victims of a 'scientific' crusade. Significantly the position of the Protestant between the oppressive occult system of Catholicism and the oppressive 'scientific' system of the British government once again expresses (is expressed in) the paradoxical position of the Ferris-texts, negotiating between the inward and the outward, the light and the darkness.

Something more disturbing for the Irish Protestant regarding this *system/occult/Catholic/'scientific state'* equation may be exposed, however, by referring to certain texts by Sheridan LeFanu which appeared in *In A Glass Darkly* in 1872, much later than the Ferris-texts but certainly expressive of one of the texts' more disturbing concerns. In 'Green Tea', the tormented Rev Jennings speaks of being 'drawn in and in, by the enormous machinery of hell' (LeFanu, 28) while in 'The Familiar', Captain Barton, equally tormented, exclaims,

> of one fact I am deeply and horribly convinced, that there does exist beyond this a spiritual world a system whose workings are generally in mercy hidden from us ... a system malignant, and implacable, and omnipotent, under whose persecutions I am, and have been, suffering the torments of the damned!
>
> (LeFanu, 57)

What these passages echo are the disquieting implications of equating the occult with the 'scientific state' and Catholicism. The occult, coinciding with the experience of these two oppressors, itself is experienced as oppressive, alien, impersonal, impenetrable. In part this is, of course, the very project of the Ferris-texts, when we recall that the texts seek to posit a realm beyond the reaches of science, a night side of nature. The disturbing conclusion of the occult becoming unknowable, however, is that its nature – whether it is benevo-

lent or evil – is put sharply into focus. Manifestations of the occult
in the tangible world perhaps prompt a judgement on this matter,
and the experience of oppression and alienation, coupled with the
experience of disorder in the world, would certainly seem to be a
cause of anxiety. Given the coincidence of the Ferris-texts with the
Famine, agrarian unrest and the upheavals of Catholic Emancipation, the Repeal Movement and the growing mobilisation of the
native nationalists, the texts might certainly express the anxiety of
the Irish Protestant about the supposed benevolence of God. The
concurrence of a deeply millennial spirit within the evangelical
movement did little to diffuse this anxiety.

We may extend this point further by positing another link
between LeFanu's text and the Ferris-texts. W.J. McCormack points
to the significance of the title of *In A Glass Darkly*, which can be seen
as a corruption of a verse from St Paul: 'For now we see through a
glass darkly, but then face to face' (1 Corinthians 13, v.12a: LeFanu,
xii). The refraction of this verse proposed by LeFanu's title seems to
propose that it is no longer possible to see through the glass.
Further, given the fact that 'glass' for the Victorians also signifies
'mirror', what appears in this 'glass darkly' is one's own face
(LeFanu, xiv-xv). This seems to suggest that the spirit world origi-
nates not from outside but from within. So far the supernatural has
been associated with the inward, but always with the inward as a
mode of perception of phenomena that originate outside. However
a disturbing subtext to the Ferris-texts is one which points to a conclusion not unlike that proposed by LeFanu's title: that it is possible
that the supernatural is created by oneself. In 'Of the Nightmare'
this question is posed:

> Have we within us the true 'devil's ladder,' or well-staircase,
> winding down into bottomless gulfs of the 'blackness of dark-
> ness' …? If we will not be afraid of ghosts, have we to be afraid
> of ourselves? (44)

In 'A few more words about Mesmerism', the culmination of the
mesmeric sleep is seen when the patient awakes 'within himself' to
a world

> out of which are projected into the external, as phantasmagory
> and magic-lantern show, shadows of mysterious realities that
> 'have their being' within. (78)

What this subtext proposes is the triumph of science, where occult
phenomena can be explained away on physiological and psychological grounds as emerging from within. Not only then may God

be evil, but in a disturbing way he may also only subjectively exist, merely finding his origin within.

At this point it is useful to introduce a concept we have not yet mentioned in our discussion of the occult, the concept of 'fear'. In 'Fireside Horrors for Christmas' we are told that the aim of the text is not 'to make the reader a better man, but merely a more uneasy one', to 'appeal to his nerves, not to his conscience' (640). In other words the project is to frighten, not to instruct. We may also usefully introduce a second term, a term employed by Freud, 'the uncanny' (*das Unheimlich*). According to Freud the uncanny effect is produced when something familiar that has been repressed is exposed, or, in other terms, when the distinction between the imagination and reality is effaced (see Freud). I have already alluded to the sense in which many of the 'metaphysical' implications of the Ferris-texts' vision of the occult were expressions, in part at least, of larger societal disorder and upheaval. More generally, Victor Sage has argued that the rise of supernatural writing from the Gothic onwards closely parallels Europe-wide movements for the Emancipation of Catholics (Sage, 28-29). What I would like to suggest is that the Ferris-texts express the uncanny effect produced among Irish Protestants for whom in mid-nineteenth-century society the imaginative/occult had suddenly been made real. This period was the era where the occult enemy, the Catholic, previously hidden and silent, became real for the Irish Protestant and began to make its collective presence felt. This presence was most tangible in the 'monster meetings' of the Repeal Association and in the emergence of the bandit-like Whiteboys and Ribbonmen, secretive initiators of rural unrest. Interestingly in 'German Ghosts and Ghostseers (II)' it is suggested that the 'puck' has 'forsaken our fields, and is become the great political leader of the day' (231), that the 'puck' has, in other words, been made real. Perhaps the most significant 'making real' of the 'imaginative', however, was in the shape of the 1834 religious census, which produced for the first time detailed figures of membership of the various churches in Ireland. For the Protestant this census proved depressing (and 'uncanny') reading, for what was written was that Catholics outnumbered Protestants in Ireland by up to four to one (Brynn, 363). For the Protestant what these statistics, monster meetings and protest movements signalled was the emergence of a huge, mobile force fearfully asserting its power on the island.

What solace, if any, do occult texts then have to offer the Protestant? I would like to suggest that occult texts like the Ferris-texts provide a covert means of exploring the imaginative as it rapidly becomes real. Given the conjunction between 'Catholic' and 'occult', the Ferris-texts, in other words, can be seen as a means of exploring the hidden, the Catholic, for analysing whether or not it is dangerous and in what way, for analysing how it may manifest itself, for mapping the extent of its power. Moreover the occult-text provides a flexible medium at one remove from the social and cultural phenomena it sets out to explore, arguably lending distance and 'objectivity' to the process of exploration, crucially permitting the Protestant to 'theorise' about the emerging Catholic 'narrative'. Further, these texts in turn permit not only this covert exploration, but also permit the Protestant define himself against an Other – in this case the distanced, different Catholic. This suggests an interesting conjunction between the occult and the Other, a conjunction I have not space to examine here.

This exploration of the Catholic/occult is played out in the Ferris-texts principally in the texts' concern with mesmerism. While striving continually to assert the validity of the occult experience beyond science, the Ferris-texts paradoxically also seek to uncover the occult and locate it in terms of magnetic and mesmeric phenomena. As we have seen, 'A Pilgrimage to Caldaro' posits a link between Catholicism and the occult. Significantly this article also argues that the phenomena encountered in Caldaro are of mesmeric origin (despite comments by the Earl of Shrewsbury to the contrary[8]). We may also draw a parallel between the mesmerist and the priest in the sense that both hold power over their patients/followers. Explorations of mesmerism then can be seen as offering a distanced means of exploring the phenomena of Catholicism, especially regarding this question of power. Moreso, however, an exploration of mesmerism offers a mode of explanation, where Catholic power can be diffused and channelled, via mesmerism, into something knowable, something which can be explained and is tangible.

It is in texts like the Ferris-texts that such channelling takes place. W.R. Wilde, in his *Irish Popular Superstitions*, first published in the *DUM*, significantly writes that 'nothing contributes more to uproot superstitious rites and forms than to print them; to make them known ... instead of leaving them hidden' (Wilde, 6). In the same way what the Ferris-texts do is write the imaginative, making it knowable, negotiable and ultimately defeatable. In other words the Ferris-texts represent the occult (because it cannot, by definition, represent itself (Marx, 254)), and thus they assume any power the occult might have. The inquiry of the Ferris-texts into Catholicism/mesmerism is thus a means, at one remove, of dispossessing the Catholic of the social, political and epistemic power he was beginning to accrue, of writing away the dark Catholic Gods of silence. At the same time, however, the writing of the imaginative makes the imaginative real – in other words, while it perhaps succeeds in diffusing one kind of fear (that of the Catholic), it creates a parallel fear at one remove, an uncanny effect produced by this very action of textualising the occult. This parallel fear reflects the uncanny effect produced by the emergence of Catholic power in the country. The exploration of this power via mesmerism then also involves an experimentation in fear, offering again at one remove a mode of exploration and explanation, this time of Protestant fear, permitting a mapping of its depth and extent. Further, this fear is necessary for, I would like to suggest, fear for the minority group is a binding force of great power, unifying disparate elements into a whole. Thus the English Protestants receive Mortimer O'Sullivan's account of *Romanism as it rules in Ireland* 'with expressions of astonishment, disgust, and horror'(O'Sullivan and McGhee, xi), exclamations which unite them in a common concern to defeat the enemy, a unity seen in the *DUM* as essential to Irish Protestantism if it is to meet its 'present dangers' (see Anon., 'How Should Irish Protestants Meet Their Present Dangers?').

IV

The dual need of the Ferris-texts to at once write Catholic power/the imaginary away, yet also to create a fear to forge Irish Protestants into a single unit, perhaps points back to the original paradox at the root of the Ferris-texts. It is very important for the Ferris-texts, as we have seen, to preserve two distinct 'occults': at once they seek to preserve a revealable occult, corresponding to the occult of the Catholic that can be exposed, detected, and diffused, and at the same time to preserve an inaccessible occult, the supernatural to which the Protestant evangelist has reference, the dwelling place of their mysterious God. Out of this inaccessible occult also arises a certain fear and anxiety, expressed in the disquieting subtexts underwriting the Ferris-texts concerning the nature of the hidden God. What is crucial is that the hidden, inaccessible occult cannot be written away. In this way, though it provides a refuge from the scientist, it is a constant source of disruption and disorder. This dark atextual silence supplies a continual cause for fear. Of the ability to diffuse Catholic power, Mortimer O'Sullivan thus writes, concerning the efforts of some Protestants:

> Little can their petty plummets sound the mighty depths of that mystery of iniquity, which cannot more easily shroud itself in a night of centuries, that it can ignite the intellectual atmosphere, and flare like a meteor through the world.
>
> (Anon., 'A New Batch of Saints', 716)

In 'Fireside Horrors for Christmas', meanwhile, it is suggested that outside the tiny ring of light from the fire there exists 'a dark and spectre-peopled void' (632), a place of darkness and terror, a source always of potential chaos. Emerging from the darkness these spectres further signify (*sign*/ify) for society and culture a connection with the 'narratives' of the past and the future, providing a model for human experience in 'narrations' that confound all vigorous attempts to 'theorise' them. In the bright, temporal text we seek to make permanent a 'now' of speaking against the darknesses of 'then' and 'tomorrow'. We write against the silences of the night side of nature.

APPENDIX 1 : THE FERRIS-TEXTS

The following are the thirty articles in the *DUM* assigned by the *Wellesley Index* to Henry Ferris, along with the evidence given in support of the attribution. References are cited in the following form: name of article, volume number of *DUM*, date of issue, page number, evidence. The numbers in square brackets are the numbers given the articles in the *Wellesley Index*.

1. 'High Cross by Bonn', 13, May 1839, 537-51. Signed 'Irys Herfner', an anagram of the name Henry Ferris. [749]

2. 'German Ghosts and Ghost-seers (I)', 17, January 1841, 33-50. Signed 'Irys Herfner'. [956]

3. 'German Ghost and Ghost-seers (II)', 17, February 1841, 217-32. Signed 'Irys Herfner'. [969]

4. 'Driftings and dreamings in various lands', 18, September 1841, 257-77. Signed 'G.H. Snogby' – see no. 5. [1028]

5. 'The two passports', 20, September 1842, 290-98. Signed 'G.H. Snogby'. Assigned by the Charles Lever records to 'Ferris'. Ferris' interest in the occult is noted. [1152]

6. 'A leaf from the Berlin chronicles', 22, November 1843, 558-68. Reference is made in this article (559) to no. 3. Also one may cite as evidence the German locale, a locale that frequently occurs in other of Ferris' writings, for example, articles 2, 3 and 5. [1283]

7. 'Mesmerism (I)', 23, January 1844, 37-53. Signed 'Irys Herfner'. [1301]

8. 'Mesmerism (II)', 23, March 1844, 286-301. Signed 'Irys Herfner'. [1320]

9. 'A few more words about Mesmerism', 24, July 1844, 78-90. Signed 'Irys Herfner'. [1368]

10. 'Of the Nightmare', 25, January 1845, 32-44. This article is full of quotations from German authors, as is no. 2. This article is referred to in no. 12 (314). Similar material is used in no. 11. [1409]

11. 'Mare's nests', 25, February 1845, 135-43. Franz Baader is quoted here (141) as in no. 2 (33). The possibility of foreseeing the future is suggested here (138) as in no. 2 (39-40). No. 12 (314) refers to this article. [1416]

12. 'A Pilgrimage to Caldaro', 25, March 1845, 305-18. Assigned by the Lever records to 'Ferris'. [1432]

13. 'More mare's nests', 25, May 1845, 527-37. The main theme of this article is mesmerism, as in articles 7, 8 and 9. [1450]9

14. 'The devil's ladder', 25, June 1845, 658-78. A story of enchantment with a German setting, ending with a ghostly voice as in articles 1 and 2. [1461]

15. 'Miscellanea Mystica (I)', 26, August 1845, 175-86. Covers similar material to articles 7-14. Uses the same format as no. 13. [1482]

16. 'Night with Mephistopheles', 26, November 1845, 570-80. German locale, as in articles 2, 3, 5 and 6. [1509]

17. 'Miscellanea Mystica (II)', 27, February 1846, 155-70. See evidence for no. 15. [1535]

18. 'Miscellanea Mystica (III)', 27, June 1846, 691-705. See evidence for no. 15. [1573]

19. 'The occult sciences – magic', 29, January 1847, 28-42. For evidence of Ferris' interest in the occult see articles such as no. 2. Also 40-42 deal with mesmerism, as do articles 7, 8, 9 and 13. [1630]

20. 'An Evening with the Witchfinders', 30, July 1847, 1-16. Refers (8) to no. 11, implying common authorship. [1688]

21. 'Another Evening with the Witchfinders', 30, August 1847, 146-61. See evidence for no. 20. [1698]

22. 'Horae Gregorianae', 30, August 1847, 224-40. Signed 'G.H. Snogby'. [1703]

23. 'Mademoiselle Lenormand', 30, November 1847, 497-510. The opening paragraph shows an obvious interest in the occult, especially in chiromancy and astrology (see no. 2). Reference is also made to animal magnetism. The Index further adds that 'the author insists that he described "the marvellous without trying to supply any rationale", which is true of everything Ferris wrote: he enjoyed the suspension of disbelief'. [1723]

24. 'Fireside Horrors for Christmas', 30, December 1847, 631-46. The opening paragraph points at once to Ferris. [1733]

25. 'A Third Evening with the Witchfinders', 31, April 1848, 440-55. See evidence for no. 20. [1768]

26. 'Night in a haunted house', 31, May 1848, 553-70. See evidence for no. 24. Also the subtitle to no. 5 can be compared to this one. [1774]

27. 'A Night in the Bell Inn', 35, June 1850, 747-52. Similar to articles 2, 26 and others belonging to Ferris. [2011]

28. `The mysterious compact (I)', 36, July 1850, 99-108. Ghost-story and German setting point to no. 2. See also evidence for no. 6. [2022]

29. 'The mysterious compact (II)', 36, August 1850, 162-74. See no. 28. [2027]

30. 'Tobias Guarnerius, a psychological tale', 37, February 1851, 225-33. See evidence for other ghostly narratives set in Germany, for example, articles 2 and 6. [2087]

As can be seen from this list, 'hard', conclusive, external evidence exists for only ten of the thirty articles attributed to Henry Ferris, namely articles 1, 2, 3, 4, 5, 7, 8, 9, 12 and 22. These attributions are made based on the deciphering of the anagrammatic name 'Irys Herfner' and the attribution of several articles to 'Ferris' in the Charles Lever records. There is little doubt that these articles were written by Henry Ferris. For the other twenty articles attributed to Ferris, however, only internal evidence is provided. This 'soft' evidence takes the form of cross-referencing between articles, most often regarding style and subject-matter. Thus article no. 10, 'Of the Nightmare', quotes German authors frequently, as does article no. 2, 'German Ghosts and Ghost-seers (I)' for which external evidence exists. 'Miscellanea Mystica', article no. 15, covers similar subject-matter, in a similar format, to articles 13 and 14, which in turn treat of similar subject-matter to articles 7, 8 and 9, for which external evidence exists.

It is, however, certainly quite possible that any author may refer to another author, especially within the close/closed circle of DUM contributors that existed. Thus attributing an article to an individual author on the basis of references from one article to another and nothing more must at least be seen as at the very least questionable. Questions have also recently been asked about an attribution procedure based on comparisons in style. In a discussion of the problems associated with assigning articles in the DUM to the like-minded brothers Samuel and Mortimer O'Sullivan, Wayne Hall takes issue with the rather ambitious use by the editors of the DUM section of the Wellesley Index of stylometric methods in assigning articles (see Hall). Hall's conclusions point towards the need for a review of the evidence for articles that are attributed based on stylometric considerations, and his proposal that uncertain attributions be qualified using such formulas as 'Unidentified. Perhaps by ...' may certainly be seen as applicable to the Ferris-texts. The evidence for articles 23 and 24, for instance, certainly appears rather tentative and calls for reappraisal.

We may also mobilise Ferris' biography in defence of a revision of the list of texts attributed to him. According to the records that exist, Henry Ferris died on 20 April 1848.[10] This places perhaps five articles under suspicion – articles 26 to 30. Though article no. 26 (May 1848) may have been in the process of publication at the time of his death, the long gap to article 27 (June 1850) indicates that possibly the subsequent four articles were not by Henry Ferris. Further, these articles ('A Night in the Bell Inn', the two-part 'The mysterious compact', and 'Tobias Guarnerius, a psychological tale') are all supernatural stories, relatively uncommon as a genre in the larger canon of writings assigned to Ferris. Certainly three ghost-stories do not appear consecutively anywhere else in the Ferris-texts, isolating these and perhaps suggesting a different author.

Given these problems of attribution, a new mode of approach to the Ferris-texts seems necessary, a mode which sees these texts as symptomatic of the concerns of a larger context rather than as creations of an individual authorial voice. In connection with this, a further mode of inquiry based in these difficulties of attribution may be suggested. Given the nature of the Ferris-texts and their concern with that which lies beyond science, the epistemic value of the 'author-function' becomes important. In his famous analysis of the author-function in discourse, Michel Foucault has pointed to the sense in which, from the seventeenth-century on, scientific discourses began to be accepted for themselves, regardless of whether or not they were attributable to an author (see Foucault). As if to bear this out, John Talbot signs his letter from Caldaro 'knowing what little authority is given to anonymous statements, especially when they relate to the mysterious' (Talbot, 42). A further line of inquiry, beyond the reach of this text here, might then be to consider the texts that are signed in the *DUM*, especially those signed 'Irys Herfner' and 'G.H. Snogby', in relation to the epistemic contexts of nineteenth-century Ireland.

APPENDIX 2 : HENRY FERRIS, A BIOGRAPHICAL NOTE

According to Burtchaell and Sadleir's *Alumni Dublinenses*, Henry Ferris, son of Barnet F. Ferris, entered Trinity College Dublin on 5 May 1817, aged 15 years. He was born in Dublin in either 1801 or 1802. He graduated, under his teacher Mr Fagan, with a B.A. in the summer of 1821 (Burtchaell and Sadleir, 278). Though listed as 'dasdanarius' (or corn-factor), Barnet F. Ferris, according to various Dublin directories for the early 1800s, was a haberdasher. His shop was located at 37 Camden Street and was later taken over by Ellen and Eliza Ferris, possibly Henry's mother and sister. 37 Camden Street was subsequently demolished and rebuilt, and is now a Chinese restaurant.

We can throw little light on Ferris' life for the period immediately following 1821. It is possible that he became an Irvingite.[11] We know that Edward Irving visited Dublin in the autumn of 1830, and attracted huge crowds with his sermons (Drummond, 121). It is probable that Ferris was recruited to Irving's circle then. Many of the Ferris-texts speak of travelling to various centres around Europe, particularly Italy (see especially 'A Pilgrimage to Caldaro', 'Horae Gregorianae' and 'Driftings and dreamings in various lands'). The texts show a familiarity with European languages and affairs. On this evidence it is quite possible that in the years after 1821 Henry Ferris travelled around Europe. It is also known that the Irvingites had very substantial communities in Germany and Switzerland (see Hastings, 425). It is possible, though not likely, that Ferris was in some way involved in these missions.

The very fact that Ferris began to contribute to the *DUM* in early 1839 suggests a disillusionment with the Irvingites. The tendency of the Irvingites towards vaguely Catholic practices has been noted by some writers (Drummond, 153-54), and the presence of Ferris' writings in the conservatively Protestant *DUM* indicates his true allegiance. A crucial passage, ridiculing Irvingite beliefs, appears as a footnote to 'Horae Gregorianae' (229). The description of the Irvingites as offering a prime example of 'epidemic insanity' displays further Ferris' rebuke of the doctrines he perhaps once held.

Henry Ferris was appointed by the Church of Ireland to a curacy at Killucan, Co Westmeath, in 1847 – the clergyman at the time was Cecil Crampton. Tragically his curacy did not last long. His parish was hit badly by the Famine, and Ferris died on 20 April 1848 of typhus while attending to his parishioners. Ferris was married, and his wife gave birth to a daughter on 4 August 1848, possibly the daughter who went on to become Mrs Bertram D'Arcy, marrying into the powerful D'Arcy family of Co Westmeath (Falkiner, 5553ff).

The last trace of Henry Ferris is in the *DUM* of January 1853 when, in a review of twenty years of the magazine's history, contributors who had since died are remembered. Ferris is remembered as 'imaginative', 'enthusiastic', and 'learned',

> skilled in strange lore: steeped in the mysteries of psychological speculation, in witchcraft and demonology, and in the biography of ghosts (Anon., 'Our Past, our Present, and our Future', 4),

the last a skill he shares with those who seek to write him back to life.

Notes

1. See appendix 1 for further consideration of the evidence for the Ferris-texts.

2. All page references to the Ferris-texts will henceforth be given parenthetically.

3. See Sage, 187-232 for an examination of the 'strange case' and its association with the theological 'case' and the legal idea of proof.

4. See also Dallas, 197-203.

5. See especially 'Horae Gregorianae', another text purporting to present an account of a visit to Italy, though much more 'dreamlike' in presentation.

6. See Sage, 26-69 for a consideration of the perceived externalisation of conscience by the Catholic and its relevance to Protestant horror fiction.

7. *The Zoist*, edited by the famous mesmerist Dr Elliotson, was published in London and ran from 1843 to 1856. Its motto, 'This is TRUTH, though opposed to the Philosophy of Ages', gives a further indication of its sense of itself under siege.

8. John Talbot (the sixteenth Earl of Shrewsbury) caused great controversy with his *Letter from the Earl of Shrewsbury to Ambrose Lisle Phillips, esq. Descriptive of the Estatica of Caldaro and the Addolorata of Capriani* which was seen to very definitely support a Catholic interpretation of the events. In a second edition of the *Letter* in 1842 Talbot refutes the idea that the phenomena have any connection whatever with phenomena produced by mesmerism.

9. 'More Mare's Nests' is reviewed briefly in *The Nation*, 17 May 1845, p.522. The author is described as knowing 'the knack of mysti-

fying people, keeping them in doubt whether he is in jest or earnest'.

10. See appendix 2 for further details of Henry Ferris' biography.

11. I am grateful to Dr Jacques Chuto for this information.

Bibliography

Anon., 'How Should Irish Protestants Meet Their Present Dangers?', *DUM* XXVI (July 1845), 114-26. Attributed to Mortimer O'Sullivan.

Anon., 'Our Past, our Present, and our Future', *DUM*, 41 (January 1853).

Anon., 'Roman Catholic Devotion – the Order of Carmel, and the Scapular of Dr Stock', *DUM* XV (March 1840), 284-94. Attributed to Mortimer O'Sullivan.

Anon., '"The Christian Remembrancer", or Arrogance Unmasked', *The Zoist* V, 19 (October 1847), 313-21.

Anon., 'A New Batch of Saints from the Vatican', *DUM* XIV (December 1839), 713-17. Attributed to Mortimer O'Sullivan.

Anon., *Conversation between Two Disciples of Mr Irving and a Clergyman of the Established Church*, _____, Dublin 1836.

Bowen, Desmond, *The Protestant Crusade in Ireland 1800-70*, Gill and Macmillan, Dublin 1978.

Boyle, Robert, 'About the Excellency and Grounds of the Mechanical Hypothesis', in *Selected Philosophical Papers of Robert Boyle*, ed. with an introduction by M.A. Stewart, Manchester UP, Manchester/Barnes and Noble, New York 1979.

Brynn, Edward, *The Church of Ireland in the Age of Catholic Emancipation*, Garland, London/New York 1982.

Burtchaell, George and Thomas Sadleir, eds., *Alumni Dublinenses, a register of the students, graduates, professors and provosts of Trinity College in the University of Dublin* (1593-1860), 2nd ed., Alex Thom and Co, Dublin 1935.

Cannon, Walter F., 'The Normative Role of Science in Early Victorian Thought', *Journal of the History of Ideas* XXV (1964), 487-502.

Carlyle, Thomas, 'Signs of the Times', in *Critical and Miscellaneous Essays*, vol.1, Chapman and Hall, London n.d., 99-118.

Crowe, Catherine, *The Night Side of Nature: or, Ghosts and ghost seers*, 2 vols., T.C. Newby, London 1848.

Dallas, A.C., *The Story of the Irish Church Missions*, Society for Irish Church Missions, London [1867].

Drummond, Andrew Lasdale, *Edward Irving and his Circle*, James Clarke and Co., London n.d.

Eichner, Hans, 'The Rise of Modern Science and the Genesis of Romanticism', *PMLA* 97, 1 (January 1992), 8-30.

Emerson, N.D., 'Church Life in the 19th Century', chap. 8 in *History of the Church of Ireland, from the Earliest Times to the Present Day*, vol.3, ed. Walter Alison Phillips, Oxford UP, London 1933.

Falkiner, W.F., 'Annals of Killucan', National Library of Ireland MS n.5422, 5553 ff.

Flew, Anthony, ed., *A Dictionary of Philosophy*, Macmillan, London and Basingstoke 1979.

Foucault, Michel, 'What Is An Author?', in *The Foucault Reader*, ed. Paul Rabinow, Penguin, Harmondsworth 1991, 101-20.

Freud, Sigmund, 'The Uncanny', in *The Pelican Freud Library, Vol. 14: Art and Literature*, ed. Albert Dickson, Penguin, London 1985, 335-76.

Hall, Wayne, 'Attribution problems: the *Wellesley Index* vs the *Dublin University Magazine*', Long Room 36 (1991), 29-34.

Hastings, James, ed., *Encyclopedia of Religion and Ethics*, vol.7, T. and T. Clark, Edinburgh 1914.

Hick, John, ed., *The Existence of God, a reader*, Macmillan, London/ New York 1964.

Hill, Jaqueline, 'The Intelligentsia and Irish Nationalism in the 1840s', *Studia Hibernica* XX (1980), 72-109.

Houghton, Walter, ed., *The Wellesley Index to Victorian Periodicals, vol. 4*, U of Toronto P, Toronto/Routledge and Kegan Paul, London 1987.

LeFanu, J. Sheridan, *In A Glass Darkly*, Gill and Macmillan, Dublin 1990.

Marx, Karl, *The Eighteenth Brumaire of Louis Bonaparte*, in *Karl Marx: A Reader*, ed. Jon Elster, Cambridge UP, Cambridge 1986.

O'Beirne, E.D., *Maynooth in 1834,* ____, Dublin 1835.

O'Sullivan, Mortimer, and R.J. McGhee, *Romanism as it Rules in Ireland*, 2 Vols., Seeley and Burnside, London 1840.

Pope, Alexander, *Poems of Alexander Pope*, selected and ed. by Douglas Grant, Penguin, Harmondsworth 1950.

Sage, Victor, *Horror Fiction in the Protestant Tradition*, Macmillan, Basingstoke 1988.

Talbot, John, *Letter from the Earl of Shrewsbury to Ambrose Lisle Phillips, esq. Descriptive of the Estatica of Caldaro and the Addolorata of Capriani*, Charles Dolman, London 1841.

Wilde, W.R., *Irish Popular Superstitions*, ed. by Seamus O'Duilearga (Irish Folklore Series), Irish UP, Shannon 1972. Appeared in the *DUM* in May and June 1849 and January and May 1850.

Williams, Raymond, *Keywords*, 2nd ed., Flamingo, London 1983.

'It is not worth telling, this story of mine – at least not worth writing. Told ... to a circle of intelligent and eager faces, lighted up by a good after-dinner fire on a winter's evening, with a cold wind rising and wailing outside ... it has gone off ... indifferent well. But it is a venture to do as you would have me. Pen, ink, and paper are cold vehicles for the marvellous.'

   J. Sheridan LeFanu, 'An Account of Some Strange Disturbances in Aungier Street', in *Victorian Ghost Stories, an Oxford Anthology*, selected and introduced by Michael Cox and R.A. Gilbert (Oxford: Oxford U P, 1991) 19-36. Originally appeared as 'An Account of Some Strange Disturbances in an Old House in Aungier Street', *DUM* XLIII (December 1853) 721-731.

Reading the Signs in Moby Dick:
Ahab's Perverse Religious Quest

Brian Cosgrove

I

Some months before he began *Moby Dick*, Herman Melville, in a whimsical letter to Evert A. Duyckinck, invoked the traditional (and ongoing) notion of the world as authored text when he referred to '"The World" – this planet, I mean' as having been 'published' by the 'Great Publisher of Mankind' (14 December 1849: *Letters*, 96). If we choose to take the statement seriously, it suggests that the world is a revelation of the Godhead: a revelation which is, of course, indirect, inasmuch as the world in its materiality is not equivalent to the Godhead, and the Godhead, if it is to be known at all, can be known only through the correct reading or interpretation of the great material (or opaque) Book. From this point of view, *Moby Dick* is concerned (at times obsessed) with the proper interpretative or hermeneutical response to this huge problematic text (the 'World'): and the well-established distinction between Ishmael and Ahab can be defined in precisely these terms. Ishmael and Ahab, in fact, embody differing hermeneutical standpoints which we might initially characterise as follows. Ishmael's reading is that of the sceptic, almost (though emphatically not quite) that of the postmodernist, who cannot expect to arrive at any sense of definitive meaning or any grasp of some (otherwise hidden) *grand récit*; Ahab's obsession, in stark contrast, is to lay hold on some such master-narrative, and to reach, in and through the teasingly symbolic order of the world, direct and unmediated knowledge of its ultimate Author. There follows from this, moreover, an inescapable paradox. Perverse and Satanic Ahab, whether blasphemous or not, is engaged in a profoundly religious quest: he embodies an archaic desire to know the sacred, even if it be the case that he defies the *numinosum tremendum*, and can only know it through that act of defiance.

II

Ishmael readily recognises that the world is an ironic one, alien and perhaps hostile to man, and as such a constant provocation to the would-be interpreter. Ishmael, however, is determined to meet such provocation with his own brand of stoicism, and pragmatically withdraws from any dispute as to the world's ultimate coherence or meaning. Hence the opening of Chapter 49:

> There are certain queer times and occasions in this strange mixed affair we call life when a man takes this whole universe for a vast practical joke, though the wit thereof he but dimly discerns, and more than suspects that the joke is at nobody's expense but his own. However, nothing dispirits, and nothing seems worth while disputing. He bolts down all events, all creeds, and beliefs, and persuasions, all hard things visible and invisible, never mind how knobby; as an ostrich of potent digestion gobbles down bullets and gun flints. (*MD*, 232)

Yet Ishmael is never consistently as insouciant as he here claims to be, and the aspiration after stoic tranquillity or apathy cannot save him from a restless speculation. He believes, at one point, that he has found his ideal of human behaviour in the savage, Queequeg, who, 'preserving the utmost serenity', is 'always equal to himself'. Surely, Ishmael adds,

> this was a touch of fine philosophy; though no doubt he had never heard there was such a thing as that. But, perhaps, to be true philosophers, we mortals should not be conscious of so living or so striving. (*MD*, 52)

Queequeg, in other words, is an instance of what Murray Krieger (in *The Classic Vision*) has termed the 'classic existent', one who accepts the given order, and unselfconsciously surrenders his otherwise isolated individuality to the larger rhythms and rituals outside the self. Yet if Ishmael has nothing but admiration for this lack of 'conscious' philosophy in Queequeg, he cannot himself lapse out of intense speculation: for he is one who must repeatedly respond to what he terms 'the problem of the universe revolving in me' (*MD*, 161). Ishmael's consciousness, in spite of his stoic attempts to create a protective carapace, is a wounded one: and in this regard he is to be distinguished from certain postmodernists, however much his scepticism might seem to have in common with theirs. For all his sporadic gestural insouciance, Ishmael never arrives at that *je m'en foutisme* which Alan Wilde sees as characteristic of postmodern irony. Nor can Ishmael wholly escape from a nostalgia for the *arche*, and thereby accept a process in which, in Wilde's summary, 'the frustation of being unable to resolve a dilemma gives way to an acceptance of the impossibility of making any sense whatever of the world as a whole' (Wilde, 44). Ishmael accepts, as a good pyrrhonist, the inevitability of his 'doubts', but his scepticism is too flexible to admit anything as absolute as 'impossibility' (a point in Wilde's argument at which scepticism tends, somewhat unsubtly, to become pure denial). Therein lies one reason for describing Ishmael precisely as a pyrrhonist rather than as a (modern) sceptic: it being arguably the case that following David Hume and others the word 'scepticism' in its post-Enlightenment manifestations has become unduly loaded with a negative bias, a spirit of denial (as in Wilde's 'impossibility'), whereas in the more ancient form of pyrrhonism one might hope to recover a more positive spirit of openness to possibility. That ancient scepticism reveals its consistency in a freedom from positivistic assertion, and need not rejoice in the banishing of the metaphysical or the religious. On such a pyrrhonist basis, Ishmael can admit into his radical uncertainty the possibility of positive 'intuitions', as in the famous summary in Chapter 85:

> And so, through all the thick mists of the dim doubts in my mind, divine intuitions now and then shoot, enkindling my fog with a heavenly ray. And for this I thank God; for all have doubts; many deny; but doubts or denials, few along with them, have intuitions. Doubts of all things earthly, and intuitions of some things heavenly; this combination makes neither believer nor infidel, but makes a man who regards them both with equal eye. (*MD*, 383-84)

A similar flexibility is evident in the eloquent acknowledgement in Chapter 114 that, even if (indeed because) we can never rest in any absolute certainty, we must continually run the gamut from faith to unbelief and back again:

> There is no steady unretracing progress in this life; we do not advance through fixed gradations, and at the last one pause: – through infancy's unconscious spell, boyhood's thoughtless faith, adolescence' doubt (the common doom), then scepticism, then disbelief, resting at last in manhood's pondering repose of If. But once gone through, we trace the round again; and are infants, boys, and men, and Ifs eternally. Where lies the final harbor, whence we unmoor no more? (*MD*, 501)

III

One reason for dwelling on the particular nature of Ishmael's pyrrhonism is to differentiate it from the scepticism of postmodernism: another, though, is to recall the affinity between Ishmael and his author Melville. The 'pondering repose of If' (a phrase in which the participial adjective destabilises the otherwise stable noun) was the only haven for Melville's own 'manhood', and one of the most revealing anecdotes in this regard is recorded in *The English Notebooks* of Melville's friend and fellow-writer Nathaniel Hawthorne. In November 1856 Melville visited his friend at Liverpool in England, and in an entry dated 20 November Hawthorne looks back to a conversation that took place eight days previously, during Melville's stay with Hawthorne at Southport:

> We took a pretty long walk together, and sat down in a hollow among the sand hills (sheltering ourselves from the high, cool wind) and smoked a cigar. Melville, as he always does, began to reason of Providence and futurity, and of everything that lies beyond human ken, and informed me … that he had 'pretty much made up his mind to be annihilated'; but still he does not seem to rest in that anticipation; and, I think, never will rest until he gets hold of a definite belief. It is strange how he persists – and has persisted ever since I knew him, and probably long before – in wandering to-and-fro over these deserts, as dismal and monotonous as the sand hills amid which we were sitting. He can neither believe, nor be comfortable in his unbelief; and he is too honest and courageous not to try to do one or the other. If he were a religious man, he would be one of the most truly religious and reverential; he has a very high and noble nature, and better worth immortality than most of us.
>
> (*Notebooks*, ed. Stewart, 432-33)

If Melville recognises (or, more accurately, 'pretty much' recognises) the impossibility of arriving at any certainty regarding the Godhead, neither can he (with a postmodern blitheness) reject out of hand all nostalgia for the absolute. His general stance, we acknowledge, recalls that of Ishmael; in addition, however, the total lack of acquiescence, and the inability to rest 'until he gets hold of a definite belief', point away from Ishmael and towards Ahab. Ahab, it might be said, embodies and dramatises (in the most extreme form) that nostalgia for absolute knowledge which Ishmael holds in check but Melville himself cannot fully suppress. It is not, therefore, surprising that Ahab should receive the kind of rhetorical endorsement he does in Melville's text: the recognition of the unavailability of certitude (Ishmael) must be supplemented by the painful yearning engendered by that baffling lack. Ahab, then, comes to represent the will to knowledge in the face of the enigmatic.

Ihab Hassan has spoken of what he terms 'the cognitive imperative', our ineradicable need 'to make sense' (Hassan, 194,196): older (and perhaps more enduring) than any postmodern emphasis on the instability of all knowledge is the assertion in the first sentence of Aristotle's *Metaphysics*, 'All men by, by nature, desire to know' (cited Hassan, 208). Part of Ahab's fascination is that he acts out this desire in its most unqualified form: surpassing Faust, Ahab tends to become a new or original prototype in his own right. And if we ask why he can be said to surpass Faust, and to speak to us in our own age more directly and more meaningfully, the answer might lie in the fact that both Ahab and ourselves inhabit a more problematic world than Faust could conceive of, a world which appears to solicit and yet simultaneously reject the most earnest hermeneutical response.

It is precisely in the problematics of hermeneutical engagement that Paul Ricoeur has discerned 'the truest expression of our modernity' (Ricoeur, *Freud*, 27). Ricoeur's own hermeneutical approach has led him, as is well-known, to a preoccupation with the nature of the symbol, and in his view our 'entire hermeneutic problem' has to do with our way of responding to the symbolic (*Freud*, 17). Since Melville inherited from the Puritan tradition and elsewhere a strong sense of ulterior meaning in all its forms (symbol, allegory, analogy and so forth), all of which feature in *Moby Dick*, the text of Melville's work obviously calls for the reader's earnest hermeneutical engagement; but, more to the point, if the World itself is a book issuing from a 'Great Publisher', then what we supremely require are interpreters who can properly decipher that much larger symbolic text. 'It is', says Ricoeur, 'in modern hermeneutics that are bound together the symbol's giving of meaning and the intelligent initiative of deciphering' ('Hermeneutics of Symbols', 45). *Moby Dick* both dramatises and stimulates this 'intelligent initiative of deciphering' *vis-à-vis* that most opaque of all symbols, the World-as-Book.

On one level at least, the white whale epitomises precisely this opacity of the world at large, and epitomises likewise the challenge to intelligent deciphering. Significantly, though, the words used by Ishmael of the whale are not 'symbol' or 'symbolic': the word in fact is one that is more problematically charged. In Chapter 68 Ishmael refers to the way in which the surface of the Sperm Whale 'is all over obliquely crossed and re-crossed with numberless straight marks in thick array', which, 'to the quick, observant eye', provide 'the ground for far other delineations'. These he proceeds to describe as 'hieroglyphical', and he recalls 'the hieroglyphics upon one Sperm Whale in particular', which he compares to 'old Indian characters chiselled on the famous hieroglyphic palisades on the banks of the Upper Mississippi'. He concludes: 'Like those mystic rocks, too, the mystic marked whale remained undecipherable' (*MD*, 314-15).

In 1822, some thirty years before *Moby Dick* was published, Jean-François Champollion (following the discovery of the Rosetta Stone in Egypt in 1799) learnt how to decode the hieroglyphics of ancient Egypt. Whatever the influential source, it is certainly the case that throughout Melville's text, as part of a sustained and more far-reaching Egyptian thematic, references to the hieroglyphical recur with an almost obsessive frequency. If we now ask what it is that the word 'hieroglyphic' connotes, then we might reply that it suggests a particular kind of difficulty for the would-be interpreter. Simply put, it both invites and refutes comprehension, decipherment; or in other terms we might describe a hieroglyph as a 'degenerate' symbol which still declares itself as a carrier of ulterior meaning but presents itself as increasingly opaque, impenetrable, enigmatic. In this respect the hieroglyph, as it functions in a text like *Moby Dick*, signals a shift from a (comparatively) naïve trust (evident in Romanticism) in the symbol as guaranteed vehicle of significance, to that sense of the symbol as something suspect or unreliable (or possibly vacuous) which is part of our modernity (think, for instance, of the quasi-allegorical procedures, or the allegory-with-no-clear-meaning, in Kafka or in some of Beckett's prose). In the early part of the nineteenth century a symbol is seen as a potent combination of the opaque and translucent, answering to Ricoeur's general description of the symbolic as a combination of 'transparency and lightness' with 'weight and opacity' (*Freud*, 49). When, in the famous passage in *The Statesman's Manual*, Coleridge pauses to provide a definition of the symbol in Romantic terms, the primary emphasis is on its 'translucence': a symbol, in the oft-quoted statement, 'is characterised by a translucence of the special in the individual, or of the general in the especial, or of the universal in the general; above all by the translucence of the eternal through and in the temporal' (Coleridge, *Church and State*, 230).[1] The hieroglyph, however, represents a step along the road away from translucence (manifest significance) and towards opacity (enigmatic significance), beyond which lies the possibility of a meaning that is either totally unavailable or (perhaps another way of saying the same thing) simply non-existent. In the broadest terms, the hieroglyphically encoded world of *Moby Dick* might be said to exist midway between the aspirational symbolism of Romanticism, and the imminent absurdism of the modern. It follows, too, that the deepest, most radical doubt in Melville's text concerns just this alternative: either the world is all-meaning, a symbol-laden text with a real (if not immediately apparent) narrative order, or else the world confronts us with a series of discrete cyphers, and is, behind its manifold phenomena, blank, meaningless and unstructured. *Moby Dick* is poised uncertainly between these contrary possibilities; such, it might be said, is the *mise en abîme* over which the text uncertainly hovers (so, too, at the end of Chapter 35, we are reminded of the way we may be said to 'hover' over 'Descartian vortices', *MD*, 162). The belief in an all-meaning world yields the recurrent reliance on allegory, 'linked analogies' (*MD*, 320), and similar tropes, such as emblematic anecdote; but this constant and energetic weaving of the text (the text itself being self-consciously fascinated with the whole metaphor of weaving and the weaver) cannot entirely conceal or screen from consciousness the other possibility, that the world is blank, meaningless, bereft of any ultimate significance.

The crucial utterance in this regard is readily indicated: it comes at the conclusion of the brilliantly sustained chapter (42) on 'The Whiteness of the Whale'. What this intense meditation on the symbolic connotations of the 'colour' white reveals is nothing less than the profound ambiguity of the world at large. 'It was', says Ishmael, 'the whiteness of the whale that above all things appalled me' (*MD*, 191), because, as he goes on to argue, our feelings towards the colour white are deeply and disturbingly ambivalent. In spite of all the accumulated associations of white with 'whatever is sweet, and honorable, and sublime, there yet lurks an elusive something in the innermost idea of this hue, which strikes more of panic to the soul than that redness which affrights in blood' (*MD*, 192).

The 'meaning' of whiteness (insofar as it can be intuited at all) is as elusive as the meaning of the whale or of life itself. At the climax of this speculative tour de force, Ishmael summons all the resources of language to attempt, finally, to articulate the sinister, suggestive something that lurks in whiteness. The sinister possibility, it emerges, is that whiteness is a stark reminder of a suspicion we would rather repress, viz., that the universe as a whole may be void of meaning: that white(=*blanc*)=blank. Why is it that whiteness should be 'at once the most meaning symbol of spiritual things', and yet 'the intensifying agent in things the most appalling to mankind'? This is Ishmael's relentless conclusion:

> Is it that by its indefiniteness it shadows forth the heartless voids and immensities of the universe, and thus stabs us from behind with the thought of annihilation, when beholding the white depths of the milky way? Or is it, that as in essence whiteness is not so much a color as the visible absence of color, and at the same time the concrete of all colors; is it for these reasons that there is such a dumb blankness, full of meaning, in a wide landscape of snows – a colorless, all-color of atheism from which we shrink? And when we consider that other theory of the natural philosophers, that all other earthly hues – every stately or lovely emblazoning – the sweet tinges of sunset skies and woods; yea, and the gilded velvets of butterflies, and the butterfly cheeks of young girls; all these are but subtle deceits, not actually inherent in substances, but only laid on from without; so that all deified Nature paints like the harlot, whose allurements cover nothing but the charnel-house within; and when we proceed further, and consider that the mystical cosmetic which produces every one of her hues, the great principle of light, for ever remains white or colorless in itself, and if operating without medium upon matter, would touch all objects, even tulips and roses, with its own blank tinge – pondering all this, the palsied universe lies before us like a leper; and like wilful travellers in Lapland, who refuse to wear colored and coloring glasses upon their eyes, so the wretched infidel gazes himself blind at the monumental white shroud that wraps all the prospect around him. (*MD*, 199-200)[2]

IV

In this way Melville's text establishes its polar oppositions: either the world is all-meaning, or it is a blank, a void. The question, like most questions in this most agnostic of works, is left unresolved (and even though, at the end of the passage just cited, Ishmael seems to offer positive advice of a typically pragmatic kind in hinting that it is better to hold on to the saving illusion of 'colored glasses' than to gaze oneself 'blind' at the nihilistic prospect, there is no larger attempt at resolution). If life does have a meaning, then it may remain to the end an 'ungraspable phantom', as Ishmael suggests in the opening chapter (*MD*, 3). As an unanswerable question, however, it continues to pivot teasingly on the ambiguous hieroglyphics (symbolical or nonsensical?) everywhere in evidence.

Initially at least, Ishmael may appear to be the ideal narrator to respond to, and devise an account of, this insoluble world; refusing to rest in any final judgement (though finding in human community what anchorage or sustenance he may, as in the secular agape or loving communion of Chapter 94), Ishmael can render something like justice to a universe which can never be reduced to stable categories. If the world is an inexhaustible and insoluble text, then on one level – the level of the pragmatic – Ishmael provides the requisite hermeneutical response in that his interpretative gestures are always sceptical and provisional.

Yet if the world is indeed symbolic (however opaquely so), then it may well (perhaps must) provoke, as part of a more genuine hermeneutical enterprise, what Ricoeur terms 'the intelligent initiative of deciphering' ('Hermeneutics of Symbols', 45: cited earlier). Ishmael's initiative is, from this point of view, hampered by his scepticism: his act of deciphering stops short of its object, and his pragmatism shields him (in a negative as well as, obviously, a positive sense) from a more risky encounter with the ulteriority of the symbol. And if we pursue this line of argument, we shall instead come to see Ahab as the more profoundly engaged hermeneuticist, one who cannot bear to remain in a state of half-knowledge, and who urges Feuerbach's 'knowledge-drive' (*Wissenstrieb*) to extremes that Feuerbach himself explicitly discountenanced. Or, from another perspective, it might be said that rather than accept the blank phenomenal world indicated in the chapter on 'The Whiteness of the Whale', Ahab as absolutist must root his being in some ultimate Power beyond the phenomenal, and create from that willed relationship a meaningful narrative for his own existence, even if the extremity of his need generates a perverse and destructive theology. The phrase that Lawrance Thompson applied to Melville – 'inverted mysticism' (Thompson, 6) – has an equal if not greater validity as applied to Ahab. For in the character of Ahab both the real hermeneutic drive and the genuine theological quest are perverted by a vindictive need to avenge himself on an ultimate power who is himself seen as vindictive and unjust.

Moby Dick as a whole indicates a number of theological possibilities (though notably excluding any orthodox Christian view), providing alternative versions of the ultimate creator of the world. One is that there is an all-powerful God who is, alas, indifferent to human affairs (as suggested in Ishmael's disturbing image in Chapter 102 of the `weaver-god' who by his weaving is `deafened, that he hears no mortal voice': *MD*, 460). Another possibility is that there is a God who is, indeed, positively benevolent but not, unfortunately, all-powerful (as hinted at in Ishmael's wry comments on Queequeg's idol, Yojo, who in Chapter 16 appears to Ishmael to be `a rather good sort of god, who perhaps meant well enough upon the whole, but in all cases did not succeed in his benevolent designs': *MD*, 70). Yet the text finally seems to dwell insistently on a third possibility, the worst theological scenario of all: that there is an inscrutable, all-powerful and tyrannical God, whose dealings with mankind are wantonly punitive and malicious.

Ahab's perverse theology, arising from his personal experience (or, more accurately, from his personal interpretation of that experience) is of this third kind, so that Ahab embodies in its most unqualified form the belief that mankind is arbitrarily victimised by some unseen Power. Ahab is (and sees himself obsessively as) a victim, having lost a limb to what he takes to be the 'intelligent malignity' of the great White Whale. 'Moby Dick had reaped away Ahab's leg, as a mower a blade of grass in the field'. No one, thinks Ahab, 'could have smote him with such seeing malice'. Ishmael as narrator adds that

> ever since that almost fatal encounter, Ahab had cherished a wild vindictiveness against the whale, all the more fell for that in his frantic morbidness he at last came to identify with him, not only all his bodily woes, but all his intellectual and spiritual exasperations. The White Whale swam before him as the mono-maniac incarnation of all those malicious agencies which some deep men feel eating in them, till they are left living on with half a heart and half a lung. (*MD*, 186-87)

The complexity of Ahab's character, then, derives from his simultaneous enactment of the roles of Faust and of Satan: the desire to know is thoroughly vitiated by the desire for revenge against the unseen Power who, through the agency of the White Whale, has maimed and baffled him. In the great utterance in Chapter 36, Ahab brings together the notions that the world is a symbolic mediation of something other, that that Other is an intelligent and malicious being, and, above all, in the ambiguous use of the word 'strike', conflates the desire for knowledge with a vindictive counter-aggression:

> All visible objects ... are but as pasteboard masks. But in each

event – in the living act, the undoubted deed – there, some unknown but still reasoning thing puts forth the mouldings of its features from behind the unreasoning mask. If man will strike, strike through the mask! How can the prisoner reach outside except by thrusting through the wall? To me, the white whale is that wall, shoved near to me. Sometimes I think there's naught beyond. But 'tis enough. He tasks me; he heaps me; I see in him outrageous strength, with an inscrutable malice sinewing it. That inscrutable thing is chiefly what I hate ... (*MD*, 167)

We can do justice to Ahab only if we can, as occasion demands, disentangle the Faustian hero from the Satanic paranoid. It is the Faustian Ahab who yearns, in Chapter 70, to learn the deepest truths from the severed head of the sperm whale: 'speak, thou vast and venerable head ... speak, mighty head, and tell us the secret thing that is in thee. Of all divers, thou hast dived the deepest ...' (*MD*, 319). Yet the chapter in which this incident occurs is (in one of the work's many Egyptian references) entitled 'The Sphynx', reminding us of the riddling nature of existence. Ahab's passion for knowledge is continually frustrated by a teasing semiosis which seems fated to remain forever indecipherable. At the end of Chapter 110, looking on the tattooed hieroglyphics on the body of Queequeg, Ahab has to live through this frustration with unusual intensity. The tattooing, we are told,

had been the the work of a departed prophet and seer of [Queequeg's] island, who, by those hieroglyphic marks, had written out on his body a complete theory of the heavens and the earth, and a mystical treatise on the art of attaining truth; so that Queequeg in his own proper person was a riddle to unfold; a wondrous work in one volume; but whose mysteries even himself could not read, though his own live heart beat against them; and these mysteries were therefore destined in the end to moulder away with the living parchment whereon they were inscribed, and so be unsolved to the last. And this thought it must have been which suggested to Ahab that wild exclamation of his, when one morning turning away from surveying poor Queequeg – 'Oh, devilish tantalisation of the gods!' (*MD*, 491-92)

V

Neither in Ishmael's (inhibited) nor in Ahab's (absolute) desire to interpret the riddle of existence do we discern what Paul Ricoeur has famously termed a 'hermeneutics of suspicion'. But it is, of the two, only Ahab who carries this desire to interpret to its logical conclusion. 'The task of hermeneutics', says Ricoeur,

> has always been ... to search for the sense under the sense, to search for the intelligible text under the unintelligible text. There is, then, a proper manner of uncovering what was covered, of unveiling what was veiled, of removing the mask.
>
> ('Critique of Religion', 215)

Insofar as he follows such a programme (whether in 'a proper manner' or not), Ahab is to be clearly distinguished from those who, like Nietzsche, Marx and Freud (Ricoeur's three masters of 'suspicion'), indulge in 'demystifying hermeneutics' (Ricoeur, *Freud*, 32, 35). Ahab's decipherment would not entail demystification: he would decode the symbol in order to experience an unmediated knowledge of the mystery. Unlike the masters of suspicion, Ahab does not understand hermeneutics as 'a demystification, as a reduction of illusion' (the sacred or the transcendent being understood as a category of the illusory); rather, he does indeed (however perversely) understand hermeneutics as 'the manifestation and the restoration of a meaning addressed to me in the manner of a message, a proclamation, or as is sometimes said, a kerygma ...' (*Freud*, 27). Fatally, Ahab's version of such a formula tends to lay a monomaniac stress on the 'me'; but the universe, for Ahab, remains a hierophany or a theophany whence he must vigorously dispel the frustrating opacity that comes between him and the ultimate Power. Moreover, when Ricoeur relates the different enterprises of Nietzsche, Marx and Freud to that of Feuerbach, he provides us with a further means of gauging the distance between Ahab and these demystifiers. It was in the first place Feuerbach, says Ricoeur,

> who said, and saw, that man was emptying himself into the absolute – that the absolute is a loss of substance. The task of man [according to Feuerbach] is to reappropriate his own substance, to stop this bleeding of substance into the sacred.
>
> ('Critique of Religion', 217)

Ishmael might, to some extent, stand for those who withhold their human substance from the sacred, in that regard agreeing with Feuerbach; but of Ahab it must be said that it is precisely an 'emptying [of] himself into the absolute' that he both desires and (perhaps) accomplishes.

All of this is an elaborate way of confirming that Ahab's quest for knowledge is also a religious quest. Within the Calvinist tradition (the version of Christianity in which Melville was reared), God is very much a hidden God, a *deus absconditus*, and the life's work of the individual is to know that God, and know also his attitude towards the individual. The following is the kind of avowal that might have come from Ahab:

> If there's ever a God in Heaven or Earth, I vow, Protest and Swear in God's strength – or that Gods [*sic*] permitting me, I'll find him out and I'll know whether he loves or hates me or I'll dye and perish Soul and Body in the Pursuit and Search.

In fact, however, this is an excerpt from the diary (dated 25 June 1744) of the youthful eighteenth century Baptist, John Collett Ryland (cited by Brantley, 75, in a context where he is dealing with the Puritan-Evangelical's personal exercise of will in the pursuit of spiritual betterment). Even though Ahab is to be differentiated from Ryland (a Baptist minister) in that he is from the outset convinced that the Creator does indeed hate him (whereas Ryland seeks the answer to that question), there is no denying the similarities of aspiration in seeking out 'God', in confronting him in as unmediated a way as possible, and in investing everything (in absolute terms) in the interests of the search. It should now seem only minimally paradoxical to describe Ahab as one who seeks a religious fulfilment.

VI

Ahab's religious quest, however, is perverted by a vindictive hostility towards his creator, and at first sight such a wilful confrontation must seem both blasphemous and suicidal. If the powers that rule the world of *Moby Dick* are benevolent (or even, as in Ishmael's weaver-god, indifferent), then Ahab is insanely self-destructive, the victim not of 'God' but of his own wilfulness. Yet, as Lawrance Thompson notoriously argued some decades ago, the text of *Moby Dick* is indeed willing to entertain the possibility that the Creator of the world is deeply malevolent and acts vindictively towards mankind; and in Thompson's view it is not only Ahab but Melville himself who 'began to resent and hate ... the seemingly tyrannous harshness and cruelty and malice of God' (Thompson, 5). Yet there is one radical qualification to be made concerning Thompson's use of the word 'God': for (whatever God Melville himself came to believe in) the God that Ahab defies is quite simply not the God of Christian (or Western) orthodoxy. Thompson was correct in suggesting that the views concerning the Creator expounded in *Moby*

Dick are 'anti-Christian'; and they are, as he also claimed, 'heretical'. Strictly speaking, however, such views are not, as Thompson further argued, 'blasphemous' (Thompson, 6-7). The views expressed by Ahab could, technically speaking, be blasphemous only if his utterances were directed against the benevolent God of orthodoxy, and such is not the case. Rather, if we move outside the orthodox theological frame of reference, and accept that the powers that rule the world are indeed malignant, inviting heroic human opposition, we can begin to see Ahab as neither blasphemous nor insane, but as doomed tragic hero, who is, moreover, representative of the whole of humanity insofar as human beings feel themselves to be victims of an unjust cosmic order.

For Ahab subsumes the archetypes not just of Satan and Faust, but that of Adam, the Biblical archetype of fallen (and suffering) man. Adam, however, is appropriated by the text from the orthodox Biblical frame, and comes to stand not just for suffering humanity, but for humanity suffering unjustly, out of all proportion to any faults committed, or even (as in the unfortunate descendants of Adam) for no fault of which they themselves are guilty.This sense of the unjust treatment of humanity may arise as a merely abstract temptation to speculative thinking, or a vague excrescence from instinctive feeling, but for Ahab the injustice is 'visibly personified' or made concrete in the figure of Moby Dick. So it is that we are told how Ahab, as heroic representative of suffering mankind, 'piled upon the whale's white hump the sum of all the general rage and hate felt by his whole race from Adam down...' (*MD*, 187). Men and women can be seen as cosmic victims, and Ahab acts as the voice of heroic protest on their behalf.

In order to accept the logic of that argument, we need to go some way towards granting the radical premise on which it depends, viz., that the Creator of the world (or of the evil in the world) is himself evil. Such a possibility is, of course, precluded by orthodox belief, but we must recognise that Melville finds room for such heterodox (and somewhat interrelated) alternatives to Christianity as Zoroastrianism, Gnosticism and Manichaeism. These three systems overlap in a profound and general sense which opposes them to Judaeo-Christian belief, as is indicated in Paul Ricoeur's distinction between two deeply-divided sets of myths regarding the origin of evil. On one side are the myths that take the origin of evil back to man (as in, for instance, the account in Genesis), making (or attempting to make) man the source of his own woes; but there are, alternatively, 'the myths that take the origin of evil back to a catastrophe or primordial conflict prior to man...' ('Hermeneutics of Symbols', 42). All three of the heterodox alternatives to Christianity mentioned above turn on just such a 'primordial conflict prior to man'.

The most ancient of the three religious systems is *Zoroastrianism*, of Persian origin, once thought to have been founded in the sixth century BC, but more recently deemed to be much older, by some six to nine centuries.[3] Zoroaster's followers are known as Parsees, a fact which contributes to the characterisation of Fedallah in *Moby Dick*. Moreover, since Zoroastrianism entailed the worship of fire, the influence of that religious system in part explains Ahab's frenzied fire-worship at key points in Melville's text. *Gnosticism* flourished (alongside early Christianity) in the second century AD. It is characterised by a determination to confront and explain the evil in the material universe, which is to say that it takes its primary religious orientation from the recognition of the existence of evil. *Manichaeism*, like Zoroastrianism is of Persian origin, and reflecting a similar doctrinal content, belongs to the third century AD. It was, in addition (and here the confluence of all three systems is in evidence) directly influenced by the mythology of Gnosticism. Finally, we know that many of the ideas associated with these religious systems would have been known to Melville through his familiarity with Pierre Bayle's *Dictionnaire Historique et Critique* (1697, 1702), an English translation of which Melville purchased in 1849, shortly before beginning work on *Moby Dick* (see Bell, 'Bayle and *Moby-Dick*', especially the summaries of dualistic theologies, 628-30, and of Zoroastrianism, 638-41).[4]

What all of these belief-systems have in common is this: that in an attempt to explain the co-existence of evil with good, they subscribe to the notion of a dual godhead or a dualistic theology. That is to say, they refer the good in the world to a benevolent power, and the evil in the world to an evil one. In Zoroastrianism, for example, Ahura Mazda, the spirit of light and good, is opposed by Angra Mainyu, the spirit of evil and darkness. Man is the focal point wherein these two primary powers wage their conflict. Equally, both Gnosticism and Manichaeism posit a dualism of light against dark, good against evil, the whole point of such dualism being to resolve an age-old theological problem. For if you allow for the existence of two ultimate principles, one good, the other evil (and the source of evil), then you are no longer faced with the option of having to attribute evil and suffering to one ultimate, benevolent God.

The recurrence of this kind of dualism in religious thinking suggests how deeply rooted it is in human experience, and how readily the ontological emotion indicated by such beliefs arises in human consciousness.[5] It is perhaps only by referring evil in the material world to an evil supernatural source that proper accommodation can be found for 'the demonism in the world', for that 'intangible malignity which has been from the beginning; to whose dominion [according to Ishmael] even the modern Christians ascribe one-half of the worlds ...' (MD, 187). For Ahab, this otherwise intangible malignity is tangibly evident in Moby Dick, in whom, as Ahab believes, 'all the subtle demonisms of life and thought; all evil' are made 'practically assailable...' (MD, 187). If elsewhere it is hinted that Moby Dick has supernatural or god-like attributes (such as his ubiquity and immortality, MD, 185), or is, as on the first day of the chase, depicted as 'the grand god' (MD, 555), we should continue to understand such references within the Manichaean and other dualistic theological schemata, for according to such dualistic theologies, it is possible to conceive of a god or a supernatural power who is indeed evil and vindictive, as Moby Dick appears to Ahab.

At the end of Chapter 116, Ahab invokes the 'dark Hindoo half of nature', deriving his own ferocious energy from that source (MD, 505). What this seems to indicate is that the creative forces which constituted Ahab, the dark powers who called him into being, have imparted to Ahab some of their own perverse energy. Later, towards the end of Chapter 119, in a modified version of Zoroastrian fire-worship, Ahab further explores this paradox, that the supernal power to which he owes his being has imparted to him that very energy whereby he may defy that power. I speak here first of all of a modified Zoroastrianism, because in Zoroastrianism proper, light or fire is unambiguously associated with the good (as in the symbol of the sun). In Moby Dick, however, light and fire constitute a richly ambiguous nexus. So it is that in Chapter 119 Ahab rejects the sun in smashing the quadrant, the emblematic sun-instrument, yet, paradoxically, continues to worship fire. The fire which Ahab worships, however, is the destructive fire of lightning which in the past has severely burnt him, leaving a livid body-length scar, which means that fire, which in the ancient Persian religious system is related to a good godhead, is here associated with its evil opposite. In Ahab's view, the lightning-fire – which we might characterise as a fire out of darkness – is a manifestation of the evil creative principle to which he owes his existence. In a speech which betrays his own deep ambivalence of feeling (dependence/defiance), Ahab acknowledges this creator as the source of his being, and at the same time offers total opposition:

> Oh! thou clear spirit of clear fire, whom on these seas I as Persian once did worship, till in the sacramental act so burned by thee, that to this hour I bear the scar; I now know thee, thou clear spirit, and I now know that thy right worship is defiance. To neither love nor reverence wilt thou be kind; and e'en for hate thou canst but kill; and all are killed. No fearless fool now fronts thee. I own thy speechless, placeless power; but to the last gasp of my earthquake life will dispute its unconditional, unintegral mastery in me. In the midst of the personified impersonal, a personality stands here. Though but a point at best; whencesoe'er I came; wheresoe'er I go; yet while I earthly live, the queenly personality lives in me, and feels her royal rights ... Oh, thou clear spirit, of thy fire thou madest me, and like a true child of fire, I breathe it back to thee. (*MD*, 514)

In the idea of an unyielding 'personality' confronting the 'personified impersonal' there is an unconditional humanist appeal of the kind found in traditional tragedy. And as Paul Ricoeur has argued, the 'tragic' arises when the human being confronts 'a "mystery of iniquity" that man cannot entirely handle', the tragic symbols indeed speaking of 'a divine mystery of evil' ('Hermeneutics of Symbols', 56). That is to say, the tragic hero is a reminder that the human individual is at the mercy of a cosmic disposition which is at best ambiguous; and, moreover, that the constant temptation for the moral imagination is to resolve that ambiguity into the simple opposition (of the kind found in Ahab's speech) between an assertive, unjustly suffering hero, and an impersonal force (usually shorthanded as 'Fate'), the very implacability of which may call forth from the suffering individual a corresponding inflexibility. It is in no clichéd sense, then, that we rightly envisage Ahab as a tragic hero. Moreover, even if our own acceptance of orthodox beliefs should establish a distance between Ahab and ourselves, his tragic appeal persists, because, inescapably, the human imagination will always be attracted to the kind of dark and radical simplification that tragedy provides ('As flies to wanton boys, are we to the gods;/They kill us for their sport...') Or, as Ricoeur has it, we are obliged to recognise that 'tragedy lives on after its double destruction by Greek philosophy and Christianity' ('Hermeneutics of Symbols', 43).

Both tragedy, then, and tragic defiance persist in their appeal to the human imagination, and it is of particular additional interest that in the rest of that outburst Ahab in fact does much to justify his defiance by appropiating from Gnosticism one of its leading tenets regarding the Creator. Addressing the lightning-fire (already established as the evil principle of creation), Ahab continues: 'There is some unsuffusing thing beyond thee, clear spirit, to whom all thy eternity is but time, all thy creativeness mechanical' (*MD*, 515). What Ahab here invokes is one of the most important beliefs in Gnosticism, this being that there is a higher, more truly spiritual divinity who exists over and above the Creator of the material world. In this crucial shift of emphasis, the dualistic theology becomes, in addition, hierarchical: and according to this view, we are acting *morally* when we defy the (lower-order) Creator and his laws, and seek instead a union with the invisible divinity who exists beyond the material universe in a state of pure (or uncompromised) transcendence. It is not he but the lower-order divinity who is responsible for the creation of our imperfect or deeply-flawed material world. (A similar concept lies behind Caliban's 'natural theology' in Browning's 'Caliban upon Setebos', where Caliban, having first envisaged a vindictive Creator-God, Setebos, arrives at the further possibility that

There may be something quiet o'er His head,

Out of His reach, that feels nor joy nor grief ... (132-33):

Caliban proceeds to characterise this pure transcendence as the 'Quiet').

We may recall also the reference in *Moby Dick*, as early as Chapter 38 (in Starbuck's soliloquy), to the 'demigorgon' or 'Demogorgon', a name that has long been thought by many scholars to be a corrupt form of 'Demiourgon', or the Demiurge. What is significant about this is that in Gnostic thought the Demiurge is precisely that inferior deity who created the material world in which suffering humanity is entrapped. (In that soliloquy in Chapter 38, Starbuck asserts that the white whale is seen by Ahab and his crew as the 'demigorgon' (*MD*, 172), an equation that once more points to Moby Dick as the visible manifestation of an evil divinity.) Beyond the material world created by the inferior Demiurge is that supreme good/God, the pure transcendence which in Ahab's term, is 'unsuffused' (unexpressed, non-manifest) in the material creation ('There is some unsuffusing thing beyond...')

Neither Ahab nor Melville, then, are necessarily to be seen as quarrelling with God, if by 'God' we mean a transcendent goodness beyond the visible creation. In that regard Lawrance Thompson got it wrong, and got it wrong in spite of his knowledge of the dualistic theological hierarchy we speak of. Thompson was aware of 'the Gnostic heresy which taught that the Maker of the material universe was not the Supreme God, but a being imperfect in power, wisdom, goodness' (Thompson, 430, in the afternotes). Yet, perhaps because he found such heretical views too repugnant, Thompson failed to follow out the consequences of such a premise, and instead collapsed his own argument into a formulaic simplicity, as in his conclusion that Melville 'went on to hate the Calvinistic concept of God, and then proceeded to hate God' (Thompson, 423). What Ahab (and possibly, but more dubiously Melville) defies is not 'God', but the Demiurge/'demigorgon' who, according to Gnostic mythology, is responsible for wrongfully mixing the emanation of pure spirit with matter, thereby creating a botched and imperfect world in which humanity is condemned to suffer. And the theological plot thickens, fascinatingly, when we recall further that the Gnostics identified the Demiurge with Jehovah the Creator. According to this (admittedly highly heretical) view, it is not only justifiable but perhaps morally necessary to defy Jehovah and his punitive and negatively restrictive laws ('Thou shalt not...': we here embark upon a line of thought that would conduct us eventually to William Blake, with his tyrannical sky-god Urizen, and his antinomian hero Jesus). If Melville felt obliged to entertain this dark and disturbingly heretical view of the Creator as harsh and punitive (though on the basis of the 'open' and 'agnostic' text of *Moby Dick* the evidence is inconclusive), it must surely have been (as commentators have frequently suggested) in defiant reaction to the Calvinist God of his youth, with his inscrutable ways and arbitrary exercise of power.

Perverse, tortured and indeed insane as he appears to be, yet, from the heterodox theological perspective of Gnosticism, Ahab might qualify not just as tragic protagonist (as argued earlier), but as moral hero. If (a very large if) the Creator of man is evil, then man is justified in defying that Creator. As always, however, in this most shifting and multifaceted of texts, it is almost impossible to bring matters to a point of closure. From a different perspective, one that pragmatically leaves the theological out of account as fundamentally unresolvable – the perspective, that is, of a humanism enlivened by a sense of man's ethical responsibility in the face of that lack of theological certainty – Ahab is indeed evil (and destructive) in his monomaniac suppression of love and compassion, love for his young wife and compassion for his fellows. The text provides the obvious contrasts: unlike Starbuck, Ahab, in spite of

Starbuck's moving appeal at the eleventh hour in Chapter 132, refuses to honour the ties of wife and child, sacred, as it were, in their human and domestic ordinariness, their relation to a humane order (*MD*, 550). Unlike Ishmael, moreover, Ahab knows nothing of loving communion with his fellow-man, a moral reality which Ishmael learns to acknowledge early on in his symbiosis with Queequeg. Ahab, it is clear, destroys in himself these sacred badges of his humanity, and destroys, moreover, along with himself, the crew committed to his care.

Only Ishmael survives to tell the tale, and we have learnt to recognise a compelling logic in this, in that Ishmael – sceptical, non-absolutist, pragmatic, enduring – has all the hallmarks of the born survivor. In a sense, too, as we have also learnt to acknowledge, the text endorses the virtues of survival, and the compromises that such survival may involve. Yet just as *Hamlet* is the story, not of Horatio, but of the Prince of Denmark, so too *Moby Dick* remains, as we have also after all come to accept, the story of Ahab, not of Ishmael: Ahab, the 'grand, ungodly god-like man' spoken of by Captain Peleg (*MD*, 83) before the voyage of the *Pequod* gets under way. One of the most subversive suggestions in Melville's great work is that man is 'god-like' in the very fact of being 'ungodly': that is to say, that he achieves his full human magnitude only in defying the unjust Creator who called him into being.

Yet even beyond that apparently terminal perception, the ambiguities begin anew. So it is that we must finally reckon whether Ahab's defiance or hatred of his 'Creator' is not also a wilful but positive desire to confront the *mysterium tremendum*, an irreversible (if perverse) attraction towards the most ultimate numinous reality he can reach, whatever guise, good or evil, that that assumes. Among his last words are these, as he is about to receive his death-blow from *Moby Dick*:

> Towards thee I roll, thou all-destroying but unconquering whale; to the last I grapple with thee; from hell's heart I stab at thee; for hate's sake I spit my last breath at thee. (*MD*, 581)

What more appropriate phrase to describe Ahab's ambition here than the one quoted earlier from Ricoeur: referring to Feuerbach's concern about man 'emptying himself into the absolute'? Is this not what Ahab, created in the increasingly faithless age of the mid-nineteenth century, is after all bent on doing? Self-destructively absolutist in his own nature, Ahab likewise yearns for a definitive and impassioned encounter with the Absolute: 'Towards thee I roll ... to the last I grapple with thee ...'

Notes

1. In the immediate context, Coleridge is in fact dealing not with 'secular' literature but with Biblical revelation, and the symbolic mediation therein of timeless and universal truths, but the trust in the symbol, and the emphasis on its 'translucence', may be regarded as indicative, at least in terms of Romantic aspiration.

2. The text has here successfully appropriated from the philosophy of John Locke the apparently abstract distinction between 'primary' and 'secondary' qualities, endowing this with a figurative power that Locke himself (distrustful as he was of metaphor and all figurative expression) would never have admitted into his own discourse. In Locke's philosophy, the primary qualities (by which he means the qualities really or truly inherent in the objective world) are extension, figure, solidity and mobility; the secondary qualities (by which he means the illusory 'imagings' of the object in our acts of perception) include colour, sound and temperature. We most easily approach these concepts through that inveterate populariser of Locke's ideas, Joseph Addison, who in *Spectator* 387 distinguishes between 'those real Qualities' which the material world actually possesses, and those other 'imaginary' qualities produced in our perception of matter. If, says Addison, we were to see only the 'real Qualities' of the material world, it would make 'but a very joyless and uncomfortable Figure'; thanks to a benign Providence, however, things are so arranged that we see that real bleakness endowed with 'imaginary' properties, so that our minds are 'cheared and delighted with agreeable Sensations' (*Spectator*, III, 209). This is the basis of Ishmael's argument at the conclusion of Chapter 42 of *MD*, though elaborated with a figurative virtuosity unknown to Addison (as to Locke); all delightful appearances are but 'subtle deceits', that overlay 'the charnel-house' of blank nature. Were we to see nature without these cosmetic 'allurements', we would be horrified by its unbearable blankness.

3. See Cohn, Norman, Cosmos, *Chaos and the World to Come*, 77, where, having cited the tradition that Zoroaster lived around the middle of the sixth century BC, Cohn adds that for more than a hundred years 'linguistic and archaeological evidence has been accumulating' in favour of the view that 'Zoroaster lived in a far earlier period, some time between 1500 and 1200 BC...'

4. In order to curtail what is already a lengthy and complex argument, I omit here all reference to the group, related to the Gnostics,

known as Ophites (or Serpent-worshippers), about whom Melville could also have learnt from Bayle. Briefly, in the myth of the Fall as recounted in Genesis, the Ophites honoured the serpent inasmuch as he had (in their view correctly) seduced Adam and Eve from servile allegiance to the Creator.

5. One reason for the persistence of Manichaean belief has to do with the difficulty in accepting that evil does indeed ultimately originate in man. So Ricoeur, having first of all established a clear disjunction between myths of evil which refer to 'a primordial conflict prior to man', and those that refer evil 'back to man', is then obliged to admit that the Adam myth, which ought properly to urge the latter option, fails to do so consistently. This inconsistency is evident in the way the Adam story incorporates, under 'the highly mythical form of the serpent' (which symbolises 'evil already there, pre-given evil'), the alternative sense that evil arises obscurely from a source that antedates man. Ricoeur goes on to argue that it is this 'invincible' sense of an evil exterior to man which accounts for the persistence of tragedy, wherein the hero is innocent as well as guilty, or is, as we might say, victimised, even if not wholly free from fault ('Hermeneutics of Symbols', 43). – Graham Greene, in our own century, confessed his attraction to 'the eternal and alluring taint of the Manichee' (*Collected Essays*, 110), though on the whole, inspired by Newman's eloquent account of the 'great aboriginal calamity' in the final chapter of the *Apologia*, he remained responsive to the more orthodox explanation of the origin of evil in the doctrine of Original Sin.

Bibliography

Addison, Joseph, Sir Richard Steele, and others, *The Spectator*, ed. Gregory Smith, 1907; repr. Dent (Everymans Library), 4 vols., London, etc., 1979.

Bell, Millicent, 'Pierre Bayle and *Moby-Dick*', *PMLA* 66 (1951), 626-48.

Brantley, Richard E., *Wordsworth's 'Natural Methodism'*, Yale UP, New Haven/London 1975.

Browning, Robert, *Poetical Works 1833-1864*, ed. Ian Jack, Oxford UP, London 1970.

Cohn, Norman, *Cosmos, Chaos and the World to Come: the Ancient Roots of Apocalyptic Faith*, Yale UP, New Haven/London 1993.

Coleridge, Samuel Taylor, *I. On the Constitution of Church and State According to the Idea of Each. II. Lay Sermons I. The Statesman's Manual II. 'Blessed Are Ye That Sow Beside All Waters'*, ed. Henry Nelson Coleridge, William Pickering, London 1839.

Greene, Graham, *Collected Essays*, Bodley Head, London 1969.

Hassan, Ihab, *The Postmodern Turn: Essays in Postmodern Theory and Culture*, Ohio State UP, Columbus 1987.

Hawthorne, Nathaniel, *The English Notebooks by Nathaniel Hawthorne. Based upon the Original Manuscripts in the Pierpoint Morgan Library*, ed. Randall Stewart, Modern Language Association of America, New York/ Oxford UP, London 1941.

Krieger, Murray, *The Classic Vision: the Retreat from Extremity in Modern Literature*, Johns Hopkins UP, Baltimore 1971.

Melville, Herman, *The Letters of Herman Melville*, ed. Merrell R. Davis and William H. Gilman, Yale UP, New Haven 1960.

— *Moby Dick; or, The Whale*, ed. with introd. by Tony Tanner, Oxford UP, Oxford/New York 1988.

Ricoeur, Paul, *Freud and Philosophy: An Essay on Interpretation*, transl. Denis Savage, Yale UP, New Haven/London 1970.

— The Hermeneutics of Symbols and Philosophical Reflection' and 'The Critique of Religion', *The Philosophy of Paul Ricoeur: An Anthology of His Work*, ed. Charles E. Reagan and David Stewart, Beacon Press, Boston 1978, 36-58, 213-22.

Thompson, Lawrance, *Melville's Quarrel with God*, Princeton UP, Princeton 1952.

Wilde, Alan, *Horizons of Assent: Modernism, Postmodernism and the Ironic Imagination*, 1981; repub. U of Pennsylvania P, Philadelphia 1987.

'Ever under
some unnatural condition':
Bram Stoker and the Colonial Fantastic

Chris Morash

I

'There is a world which is indeed our world'. It is, writes Tzvetan Todorov in *The Fantastic*, 'a world without devils, sylphides, or vampires'. There are, however, moments when literature presents us with 'an event which cannot be explained by the laws of this same familiar world'. When this occurs, Todorov argues, we must hesitate, and ask if the event is simply an 'illusion of the senses', or if, on the other hand, 'the event really has taken place'(25). On the basis of these two options, he proposes a generic subdivision of the literature of the supernatural which has influenced almost all subsequent critical debate in the area. If, in the first case, an apparently supernatural event can be shown to have a natural explanation, we are dealing with a literary genre which Todorov calls the 'uncanny'. For instance, examining the body of the phantom beast in the final episode of *The Hound of the Baskervilles*, Holmes and Watson realise that it is simply a large dog coated in a 'cunning preparation' of phosphorus (Conan Doyle, 284); in such a case, the supernatural is revealed as a misrecognition of the natural. Todorov distinguishes this type of fiction from a second genre, the 'marvellous', where the supernatural is a given condition of the text: 'In a hole in the ground there lived a hobbit' (Tolkien, 1). In the world of *The Hobbit*, hobbits, elves and wizards simply exist; their ontological status, at least within the world of the text, is not subject to question.

As different as these two genres may appear, they share one important similarity. In uncanny tales such as *The Hound of the Baskervilles*, while there is doubt about the status of the supernatural throughout much of the story, the laws of the natural world commandingly reassert their authority in the final pages. A spectral monster may run rampant for thirteen chapters, but in the end we are reassured that luminescence can only be produced by phosphorus. Marvellous fiction, by contrast, is typically concerned with constructing its own laws. The opening pages of *The Hobbit*, for instance, supply its readers with details of the physical characteris-

tics, size, lifespan, social organisation, and living quarters of hobbits. Unlike the uncanny, however, the marvellous does not use the
dialogism of the novel's form to juxtapose its own laws with the
laws of the reader's world. By setting down its own exclusive conditions in its opening pages, the marvellous tale gives the reader no
opportunity to hesitate in the presence of the supernatural and ponder
its ontological status. Consequently, the laws of the natural world
may be put in abeyance, but they are not contradicted. They are
simply tucked away, safe and sound, for the duration of the reader's visit to Hobbiton. In short, this means that both the uncanny
and the marvellous, in their different ways, reinforce rather than
question the concept that the world is governed by stable, knowable laws.

There are, however, literary texts which hover uneasily between
the two certainties of the uncanny and the marvellous, creating an
agnostic limbo of the undecidable which Todorov calls the 'fantastic'. The text usually cited in this context is Henry James's *The Turn
of the Screw*. Is the governess subject to hallucinations, or is she really
seeing ghosts? If the text fully endorsed one or the other of these
interpretations, it would be either uncanny (in the former instance)
or marvellous (in the latter). As it stands, it is both and neither, a
textual instance in which, as James puts it in his preface, there is
'not an inch of expatiation'(42), and the binary opposition of natural
and supernatural is unwritten.

In the twenty-five years since the first publication of *The
Fantastic*, Todorov's generic distinctions have identified the decon-
structive moment of the fantastic as an important, if elusive, aspect
of the writing of the unreal.[1] Christine Brooke-Rose, for instance,
finds Todorov's concept of a genre of the fantastic to be 'an extremely
useful working hypothesis', but wonders why it is impossible to
find so few pure examples that fit the definition (71). This leads her
to suggest that we should modify Todorov's definition of the fantastic as a genre in which 'the reader's hesitation between natural
and supernatural explanations of apparently supernatural events
must be sustained to the end'. Instead, she suggests, 'the pure fantastic is not so much an evanescent genre as an evanescent element;
the hesitation as to the supernatural can last a short or a long
moment and disappear with an explanation' (Brooke-Rose, 64). As
such, the indeterminacy which characterises Todorov's fantastic
can be understood as a structural feature of almost all supernatural
fiction, present or absent in varying degrees.

'The fantastic', then, to use Todorov's formulation, 'is that hesitation experienced by a person who knows only the laws of nature, confronting an apparently supernatural event'(25). Whether understood as a genre or as a structural element, however, there is a foundational assumption in Todorov's definition which it is worth examining further. It could be argued that the length of time which a literary text requires to dispel the moment of the fantastic is a measure of the degree to which that text suspends knowledge of 'the laws of nature'. Such a suspension may, of course, take the form of a game. James admits as much in his preface to *The Turn of the Screw*, describing it as 'a piece of ingenuity pure and simple, of cold artistic calculation, an *amusette* to catch those not easily caught' (38). Equally (and perhaps more importantly), it may act as an index of a real inability to use the discourse of the natural at a particular cultural moment. To put it another way, the existence of fantastic fiction in a society may well be indicative of a situation in which the opposition between the natural and supernatural collapses, and a third condition of unknowing emerges. If the literary form of this epistemological abyss is the fantastic, its disruptive ability to prise apart the natural/supernatural binarism suggests the term 'unnatural'.

The unnatural, then, is a condition in which those 'laws of nature', with which Todorov assumes the reader's intimate acquaintance, appear unfamiliar. But what do we mean by 'the laws of nature'? Perhaps the best place to begin a brief genealogy of the discourse of 'the laws of nature' is in the opening pages of Newton's *Principia*, which state that the world operates according to knowable natural laws. 'The whole burden of philosophy', writes Newton in the Preface to the 1686 edition of the *Principia*, 'seems to consist in this – from the phenomena of motions to investigate the forces of nature, and then from these forces to demonstrate other phenomena' (1). Of course, Newton was writing primarily about the natural laws which govern aspects of the material world such as gravity, planetary motion and optics. However, in the eighteenth century this concept of 'laws of nature' was extended metaphorically to the operations of society in texts such as Hume's *Treatise of Human Nature* of 1748, and is later developed not only by writers as diverse as Kant and Fourier, but also through the explosive growth of the discourse of political economy in the nineteenth century. The effect of this discursive proliferation was such that by 1849, for instance, it was possible for the author of an anonymous pamphlet published in London with the title *Pauperism: Is it the Effect of a Law of Nature* to state that 'it is assumed as a principle throughout the following Essay, that everything in this world, moral and physical, is governed by certain fixed human laws, established by Providence, known in common language as the Laws of Nature' (1).

It is worth noting that this anonymous text not only asserts that 'certain fixed human laws' are known in 'common language' as the Laws of Nature; it also maintains the insistence on providential origin with which Newton begins his *Principia*. In a similar vein, James Taylor's *Political Economy Illustrated by Sacred History*, published in 1852 argues that 'the early portion of Sacred History ... is the history of a people emerging from a state of comparative barbarism, and under the influence of divine principle, progressing in the arts of civil government' (13). What Taylor and our anonymous pamphleteer are doing here is by no means unique, and can be found in the work of their better-known contemporaries such as Spencer or T. H. Huxley; they are claiming that the expansion of the scientific state, and the development of a society from 'barbarism' to 'civil government' is not only natural, but providential. The dark corollary of this, as the *Pauperism* pamphlet spells out, is that it can not have been 'intended and decreed by providence that an extensive able-bodied pauperism should form a necessary part of a civilised society'. Poverty, therefore, is caused by 'nature being thwarted in her operations' (25); it is unnatural, contrary to the laws of Nature, which are the laws of God. Poverty, in such a regime of truth, is evil.

In the case of Victorian Ireland, this extension of the laws of nature to the civil sphere was traumatic and disruptive. The economist Nassau W. Senior, for instance, writing of the Irish Famine in the *Edinburgh Review*, begins by claiming this principle of natural social law as his foundational assumption:

> We are ready to admit that the example of England must materially affect all Irish questions. There exists throughout the civilised world a principle, somewhat resembling that of gravitation, which enables the institutions, the customs, and even the conduct of separate countries to influence the conduct, customs, and the institutions of every other (210).

Just as in 1857 Herbert Spencer was to compare 'this law of Progress, in its multi-form manifestations' with the Newtonian 'law of gravitation'(30), Senior is here suggesting that English customs and institutions should be effective in Ireland, in accordance to a natural law 'resembling that of gravitation' which exists 'throughout the civilised world'. The problem he encounters when applying this to a country in which poverty had reached catastrophic proportions can be seen a few pages later in the essay, when he writes that in Ireland the consequence of the failure of the potato crop 'was Famine – a calamity which cannot befall a civilised nation; for a civilised nation, as we remarked before, never confines itself to a single sort of food' (222). The natural laws of social development may exist for Senior 'throughout the civilised world'; the famine of the 1840s, however, placed Ireland for him beyond the pale of that civilised world. As a consequence, his argument that the institutions and customs of England should be applicable in Ireland collapses, and its foundational assumption of an immutable law of social development is undermined, shorn of its universality. It is as if, for Senior, it were discovered that there were spots on the earth in which there was no gravity.

For proponents of progress as a natural law in the second half of the nineteenth century, therefore, the case of Ireland whispered the dangerous possibility that the laws of nature were neither fixed nor unchanging. Moreover, we can see this fearful awareness not only as something produced by writers located in the metropolitan centre of culture, such as Senior; we can also see it internalised by Irish writers of the period, who often seem to view the laws of nature, and particularly progress as a law of nature, through a lens of estrangement. 'Of all the wide world', wrote the bourgeois nationalist newspaper, *The Nation*, in 1851, 'ours is the only country we know of that, during this decade, has retrograded in the scale of national strength, happiness, and liberty' ('History of Ten Years', 728). For many members of the Irish middle classes, progress was natural (or so they were told); but it was also something which happened elsewhere. As a consequence, Ireland becomes the site of the unnatural in the Victorian order of things, as *The Nation* recognised with bitter sarcasm in 1848:

> Ireland is the fatigue-ground of English imagination, and a full-bellied, dyspeptic people must have some daily providence of terror, that they may 'sup full of horrors', and bless their stars for living east of the channel. Every people in every age have had their country of monsters, where the human kind, like evil demons, drank human blood, and lived on the marrow of dead men's bones. [...] Mrs Anne Radcliffe being dead, [...] it is now our part to furnish England with monsters, thugs, and 'devils great and devils small' ('Priest-Hunting', 89).

II

Number 15, Marino Crescent, where Bram Stoker was born in 1847, is in one of Dublin's leafier suburbs, overlooking Dublin Bay;[2] it does not look like it was once part of a 'country of monsters' where human kind 'drank human blood and lived on the marrow of dead men's bones'. Nor was there much evidence of the monstrous in the family. Stoker's father, also named Abraham, was a civil servant in Dublin Castle, and the solidly middle class family were members of the Church of Ireland. Stoker, after a sickly childhood, did the expected thing for a member of Dublin's Protestant middle class in the last century, and attended Trinity College, Dublin. While in college, his abilities as an orator won him recognition, even in the company of fellow students of the calibre of Standish O'Grady, Oscar Wilde and Edward Carson,[3] and during the 1872-3 academic year Stoker became Auditor of the prestigious College Historical Society, or 'Hist'. From auditorship of the 'Hist', it was but a short step to a middle-ranking post in the Irish civil service.

However, as one reads through Stoker's written work, from his earliest experiments in prose fiction in the 1870s, through his best known work, *Dracula*, in 1897, to the journalism and fiction written in the years just before his death in 1912, a complex and fraught dialectic emerges between a frantic endorsement of progress as a natural law of social development, and its dark alternative, atavism, barbarism, chaos. For instance, standing up in the Dining Hall of Trinity College to deliver his Auditor's Address on a Wednesday evening in November of 1872, Stoker told his fellow students, the assembled officials of the College and the Society's patron, Sir James Napier, that 'everything sinks and falls in time but nothing is eternal but Truth and Progress. These are abiding principles which no force can stem or stay' (*Address*, 32). There is something less than resounding in the syntax of this statement. Indeed, prefacing the assertion that 'nothing is eternal but Truth and Progress' with the contradictory statement that 'everything sinks and falls' has the effect of erasing both statements, momentarily unwriting the narrative of progress.

Stoker's anxieties here about the irreversible trajectory of progress prefigure more widespread concerns later in the century, particularly in the fear that 'society, as it exists amongst us, both political and social, is rapidly becoming effete' (*Address*, 15). This anxiety that the relentless improvement of material comfort would eventually produce an enervated society would, for instance, take

an influential literary form in H.G. Wells's *The Time Machine* of
1895, and begins to appear even in the late works of formerly fer-
vent apostles of human perfectibility, including Herbert Spencer.
Stoker prefigures this widespread malaise of the 1890s in the
Dublin of 1872, bringing together two loci of anxiety which will
continue to mingle uneasily throughout his fiction: sex and race.
Early in his Historical Society *Address*, he declares that 'the only
hope which remains for its [society's] regeneration is that we may
yet be able to carry into it some of that personal purity which still
exists with individuals' (*Address*, 15). Here we have the first hints of
the obsessive concern with sexual purity which so many critics
have identified in *Dracula*,[4] which is such a prominent feature of
novels like *The Jewel of the Seven Stars*, and which would become
dogmatic in his later journalism. Indeed, in 1908 we find him calling for censorship which is 'continuous and rigid' in relation to literature dealing with 'the only emotions which in the long run harm,
those arising from the sex impulses'('Censorship', 483). 'If progress
be a good', he writes in 'The Censorship of Fiction', 'the power of
evil, natural as well as arbitrary, must be combatted all along the
line' (481).

In Stoker's 1872 *Address* the idea of 'personal purity which still
exists with individuals' makes a metaphorical leap not uncommon
in the latter half of the nineteenth century; it becomes equated with
racial purity. Or, more precisely, it becomes associated with the
idea that certain races, because of their isolation from the progress
of European culture, have remained 'pure', untainted by the 'effete-
ness' which is progress's emaciated twin. It has been argued that
this fear of racial degeneration is at work in *Dracula*, as the Count
boasts to Jonathan Harker that the blood of Attila the Hun runs in
his veins, and 'the glories of the great races is as a tale that is told'
(*Dracula*, 43). Cut off from the modernisation of European society in
his Balkan mountain fastness,[5] Dracula's blood remains pure. For
the Bram Stoker who addressed the Historical Society in 1872, however, the race which had resisted the degenerative effects of
progress was the 'Celtic race'. 'Ireland in all her suffering of centuries has gained this one advantage', he tells his listeners. 'Her people have remained the same whilst other peoples have slowly
changed for the worse'. As he develops this theme of an ancient,
unchanged people emerging into the modern world to regenerate
it, we can see the figure of Count Dracula, last remnant of an
ancient, isolated race, taking form. This becomes particularly
apparent when we remind ourselves that the same month in which

Dracula was published – May of 1897 – also saw the first Feis Ceoil and the first Oireachtas; Sigerson's *Bards of the Gael and Gall* followed a few weeks later. 'Unless my senses deceive me', notes Jonathan Harker in Dracula, 'the old centuries had, and have, powers of their own which mere "modernity" cannot kill' (51). 'And now', Stoker declared in 1872, 'amongst these others comes forth this old-world people – seeming half barbarous amid an age of luxury, but with strength and pride intact, and claims its position, as, at least, their equal' (*Address*, 29-30).

For a member of Dublin's Protestant middle class in the 1870s, the prospect of a half-barbarous Celtic race returning 'amid an age of luxury' to claim its position was a prospect to be viewed with mixed emotions. On one hand, Stoker's position echoes Matthew Arnold's lectures *On the Study of Celtic Literature*, published five years earlier. 'It is a consoling thought', Arnold writes, 'and one which history allows us to entertain, that nations disinherited of political success may yet leave their mark on the world's progress, and contribute powerfully to the civilisation of mankind' (ix-x). Arnold's Celts, 'out at elbows, poor, slovenly, and half-barbarous', lacking 'the skilful and resolute appliance of means to ends which is needed to make progress in material civilisation', nonetheless have a role to play in bringing 'sensibility' back to British culture (88, 90). Aubrey De Vere was thinking in similar direction as early as the 1840s, when he noted that 'over-civilisation, a thing as opposed to Humanity as barbarism' has made the hearts of religious believers 'hollow and sucked the Spirit out of their minds' (NLI MS 3747). For De Vere, as for Arnold and, indeed, Yeats later in the century, Ireland's lack of material progress was proof of a spiritual destiny to regenerate an 'over-civilised' world from which the spirits had fled.

On the other hand, it is worth remembering that Michael Davitt opens *The Fall of Feudalism in Ireland* with a passage from Edmund Spenser which mobilises this same narrative of Ireland's savage resurgence in the form of a threat. 'Perhaps', begins the passage, 'Almighty God reserveth Ireland in this unquiet state stille, for some secret scourge which shall by her come unto England; it is hard to be knowne, but yet more to be feared' (3). Between Arnold and Davitt, the ambivalence of the concept of the Celtic race as a barbarous remnant in an enervated civilised world becomes apparent. For Arnold, the revival of Celticism is part of 'the fusion of all the inhabitants of these islands into one homogeneous, English-speaking whole … to which the cause of things irresistibly tends' (10).

For Davitt, the return of the Celt is part of a power struggle whose tide has turned. Davitt accepts the dominant narrative of history as progress from feudalism to democracy – as his title, *The Fall of Feudalism*, suggests. His Celts, however, have 'a persistency of purpose and a continuity of racial aim not associated by English or other foreign critics of Celtic character with the alleged mercurial spirit and disposition of the Irish people' (xiii). Davitt's Celts have the efficiency and determination of modernity, combined with the energy and ferocity of past centuries.

When Stoker told his listeners among the College Historical Society that 'the Celtic race is waking up from its long lethargy, and another half century will see a wondrous change in the position which it occupies amongst the races of the world' (28), both Stoker – whose parents were both of English ancestry – and his predominantly Protestant audience would have been aware that the Celtic race was something from which they would have been excluded by many of their countrymen. It should therefore come as little surprise to find that 'old-world' races, 'with strength and pride intact', return to trouble the present with an obsessive frequency in Stoker's fiction, whether in the form of the Count in *Dracula*, or ancient Egyptians in *The Jewel of the Seven Stars* of 1903. Indeed, the paralysing force of this anxiety can be registered in the fact that this same metanarrative informs his last novel, *The Lair of the White Worm*, published in 1911, and is equally present in one of his very earliest pieces of published fiction, 'The Chain of Destiny', written for a nationalist penny weekly, the *Shamrock* in 1875.[7] The tale's hero, Frank, staying in a remote country house, The Scarp, must confront a shadowy, supernatural creature known as 'the phantom of the Fiend' – 'a sort of shadow with a form' ('Chain', 499) – before he can marry Diane Fothering, a woman with whom he is in love, but has never seen. Upon meeting Diane, he realises, in a plot twist which echoes Sheridan Le Fanu's 'Carmilla' published three years earlier, that she is the double of a woman whose portrait hangs in the big house: 'we found in strange old writing on the grimy canvas a name and date, which, after a great deal of trouble, we made out to be "Margaret Kirk, 1572"' ('Chain', 514). Here, refracted through the conventions of gothic fiction, are the 'old centuries' returning, both as a shapeless, devouring terror which threatens to destroy the future – 'To-morrow and to-morrow, and to-morrow, the fairest and the best', taunts the phantom (499) – and as the beloved in the present, the object of a forcibly restrained desire.

The specifically Irish dimension of this neurotic narrative of a predatory past becomes apparent seven years later in 1882, with a collection of stories ostensibly written for children, *Under the Sunset*. One of the tales in this collection, 'The Invisible Giant', is based on an account by Charlotte Stoker (Bram Stoker's mother) of the cholera epidemic in Sligo in 1832. 'In a very few days', she writes, 'the town became a place of the dead. No vehicles moved except cholera carts or doctors' carriages. Many people fled, and many of these were overtaken by plague and died by the way' (Farson, 14; Ludlam, 26).[7] Stoker's refiguration of this account is set in a congested city, in which there are 'many great old houses, story upon story high, and in these houses lived much poor people' (*Sunset*, 47). Beyond the borders of the city are marshes: 'Death has many children, and there are Giants in the marshes still. You may not see them, perhaps – but they are there' (*Sunset*, 47). Taking a 'vast shadowy form' (or, more precisely, an absence of form) akin to Stoker's earlier 'phantom of the Fiend', one of these Giants invades the city, his 'great arms [...] outspread, veiled in his robe, till far away the shroud was lost in the air [...] the face was that of a strong man, pitiless, yet without malice; [...] the eyes were blind' (*Sunset*, 55). Stalking invisibly through the marketplace, he lays his hands on random individuals, who writhe in pain, turn black, and die. At the tale's end, the Giant retreats back into the marshes, and the little girl who has watched his depredations hears 'the echo of the words: "Innocence and devotion save the land"' (71) drifting to her in the wind.

There are several aspects worth attending to in this strange narrative. In the first place, there is the obsessive concern with purity which runs through Stoker's work, here manifested in the enigmatic ending; precisely whose 'innocence and devotion save the land' is never quite made clear, although the phrase does echo Stoker's plea for 'individual purity' in his Historical Society Address a decade earlier. Perhaps more problematic, however, is the manner in which the text works with the conventions of literary allegory. When, in the tale's final lines, Stoker refers to the agent of death as 'the great shadowy Giant Plague' (71), he is signalling that the story is to be read as an allegory. On one level, the Giant is not really a giant at all; he is second-level signifier for disease. Moreover, when Stoker tells his readers that 'it was only when the town began to get thinned that people thought of the vast numbers that had lived in it' (66-67), he is locating his allegory in what was (and still is) a very modern discourse of demographic change, Malthus's principle of population. Were it not for famines, plagues and wars (or the fear of these things), Malthus had argued, population would grow beyond its ability to support itself. As such, plagues act as an agency of progress, insofar as they thin an overcrowded population and allocate a larger share of existing resources to those who survive. At the same time, however, as we saw with Nassau W. Senior, the existence in a society of famine or plague disrupts the narrative of progress; such things are simply not supposed to happen in civilised societies which conform to the laws of nature. 'In the earlier periods of the history of modern Europe', writes Malthus, 'plagues, famines, and mortal epidemics were not infrequent, yet, as civilisation and improvements have advanced, both their frequency and their mortality have been greatly reduced, and in some countries they are now almost unknown' (Malthus, 254). According to the laws of progressive material improvement, famine and plague are remnants of a medieval, indeed, a biblical past. And yet, in Stoker's lifetime, famine and plague were a recurring feature of Irish life. Indeed, while Stoker was writing *Under the Sunset* in the winter of 1879-80 an economic depression and a series of crop failures were producing conditions which in some areas matched those of the late 1840s.

If we treat Stoker's Invisible Giant as an allegory for plague, it is worth keeping in mind Todorov's observation that 'the fantastic is effaced by allegory' (68). Hence, at one level of reading, Stoker's 'The Invisible Giant' escapes the state of ambivalent signification which is the fantastic by allowing the reader to interpret an apparently supernatural event as a coded reference to a real event. However, if the works of an author constitute a genre in their own right (as can be argued in the case of a writer like Stoker, whose concerns are so obstinately uniform), there is something which unsettles this tidy explanation. Yes, the formless giant in 'The Invisible Giant' is an allegorical figuration of plague; but the same signifier, a formless, invisible giant, also appears in 'The Chain of Destiny', where it has no obvious allegorical function. Moreover, in Stoker's later fiction, Dracula is described as having the ability to take a similarly formless, gigantic shape, similarly visible only to a select few. Hence, when we find the same signifier connected both to a natural signified (plague) and to a supernatural one (the 'phantom of the Fiend', the vampire), we are entering a textual space in which the distinction between the natural and the supernatural is no longer clear. In the case of 'The Invisible Giant', this can lead us to identify an instance of the fantastic which is not effaced by allegory, but which can be said to inhabit it. The Giant is an allegory for plague. Famine and plague have, as Malthus, Senior and others would maintain, no place in the modern, progressive order of which Stoker was such an ardent, if troubled, advocate. Yet both had taken place in Ireland in Stoker's lifetime. Hence, both real and unnatural, both an agent of progress and an index of its absence, plague in 'The Invisible Giant' forces us to hesitate, not at the level of the signifier, but at the level of the allegorical signified; in so doing, we find ourselves in the realm of a fantastic so intense that it effaces, instead of being effaced by, allegory.

III

The fantastic came looking for Stoker, it would seem, rather than the other way around. In almost all of his texts there is a struggle to write into discourse that which threatens to elude representation; he is not courting epistemological ambivalence, it could be argued, but calling it up so that it may be entered into language and controlled. Indeed, although it may appear anomalous, Stoker's first book can act as a paradigm in this regard. *The Duties of Clerks of Petty Sessions in Ireland*, published in 1879 while Stoker was working in Dublin Castle, is an attempt to regularise clerical duties in the Petty Sessions. In his introduction, Stoker admits that while he is attempting to formulate 'a great and effective system of procedure which must sooner or later be adopted for the whole British Empire', it is possible that 'many things may have been forgotten or passed over in ignorance'. This he attributes to 'the difficulty in collating the accumulated facts and theories resulting from the operation of the last twenty-seven years' (vi). If the Empire was to continue to expand, bringing with it the benefits of natural progress and order, these unknown areas of administrative procedure needed to be controlled; and yet, the very act of attempting to control the imperial administration's own dark spots conjures up an ever-receding horizon of 'things forgotten or passed over in ignorance'. Only two years before *The Duties of Clerks of Petty Sessions* was published, a bewildering array of Irish courts – Queen's Bench, Common Pleas, Exchequer, Admiralty, Probate and Divorce, and Chancery – had been amalgamated into a single supreme court of judicature (Vaughan, 471); in regularising one part of this new, labyrinthine Irish legal system, Stoker evokes all of those aspects of court procedure which remain uncharted. And, through Stoker's expressed wish that his procedure be applied to the whole Empire, he conjures up an ever-receding horizon of the legal systems of

India, Australia, Natal, Singapore, Burma, Egypt, and the rest of the expanding imperial administrative apparatus. Hence, as the knowledge of Empire multiplied, so too did the things liable to be 'forgotten or passed over in ignorance', the unknown increasing proportionally with the known.

Stoker's attempt to regularise clerical procedure in the Petty Sessions forms a part of what Thomas Richards has usefully defined as the 'imperial archive' – 'a fantasy of knowledge collected and united in the service of state and Empire' (6). Indeed, while Richards seems unaware of Stoker's work as a civil servant, he has argued in relation to *Dracula* that as a figure capable of changing his form, the vampire 'poses a direct threat to the order of things and, by extension, to the general order of an empire figured as knowable within a Darwinian frame of comprehensive morphological knowledge' (59). That system of naming and classifying the natural world, which, as Foucault has argued, 'covers a series of complex operations that introduce the possibility of a constant order into a totality of representations' (Foucault, 158), forms part of the same *episteme* which makes possible the archive of the scientific state, and, by extension, the empire. Hence, for Richards, *Dracula* is a novel in which a being who threatens to disrupt the possibility of 'morphological knowledge' is defeated by that which he challenges, 'a smoothly functioning imperial archive' (64). It is, he maintains, the dense web of telegrams, transcripts, letters and books which pass back and forth among the vampire hunters, which constitutes the nemesis of the vampire.

In Richards' reading of *Dracula*, pitting the Count against the imperial informational order, the vampire 'is clearly a feudal lord', and as such represents 'the recrudescence of an obsolete form, absolutism', which must be overcome by an 'emphasis on the positive form of knowledge' (63) if the imperial project is to retain its coherence. Without denying the interpretative force of this reading, it should be read in conjunction with Jennifer Wicke's 1992 essay, 'Vampiric Typewriting', which recognises that not only Van Helsing and his band of vampire-hunters use the cutting edge of information-retrieval in the text, for Dracula himself owes much of his power to his immersion in the modern informational order. When Jonathan Harker first encounters the Count in his Translyvanian castle, for instance, the vampire is surrounded by 'books of the most varied kind – history, geography, politics, political economy, botany, geology, law ... the London directory, the "Red" and "Blue" books, Whitaker's Almanac, the Army and Navy

Lists, and ... the Law List' – 'my good friends', Dracula calls them (*Dracula*, 30). Dracula, argues Wicke, 'must come to London to modernise the terms of his conquest, to master the new imperial forms and to learn how to supplement his considerable personal powers by the most contemporary understanding of the metropolis' (487). It is not, she goes on to argue, 'merely the atavism of Dracula that makes his appearance in England so frightful; it is his relative modernity' (490). In short, Dracula is not simply a sign of 'the power of the old centuries'; he is equally a sign of the proliferating knowledges of modernity.

'Remarkably enough', writes Wicke, 'I would suggest that Dracula experiences some of the poignant sense of estrangement of the colonial intellectual' (488), insofar as he has mastered the forms of modernity, but is still treated as a primitive anachronism. This might appear less remarkable if Wicke did not consider *Dracula*, as she announces at the beginning of her essay, as 'the first great *modern* novel in *British* literature' (467). The italicisation of 'modern' is Wicke's; the italicisation of 'British' has been added, to which might be appended a large question mark. For, if we restore *Dracula* to a context of Irish writing, by recalling that it was written by a member of the Irish intelligentsia who had worked for the British imperial administration, then both the paradoxical coexistence of atavism and modernity in the same figure, which Wicke notes, and the similarity of such a contradictory state to 'the poignant sense of estrangement of the colonial intellectual' becomes less remarkable; indeed, one is almost tempted to say that it appears 'natural'.

In Stoker's early writing, such as the *Address to the College Historical Society* in 1872, there is still a lingering hope that the unruly powers of the past might be transformed by a modern market economy. 'The very same individuality and self-assertion and passionate feeling which prompt to rebellion and keep alive the smouldering fires of disaffection', Stoker said of Ireland on that occasion, 'become shrewdness, and enterprise, and purpose in commercial prosperity' (*Address*, 29-30). However, twenty-five years later, the Dracula who questions Jonathan Harker on whether it is possible to retain two lawyers, and who is found by Harker at one point 'lying on the sofa, reading, of all things in the world, an English Bradshaw's Guide' (*Dracula*, 34), can be read as an articulation of the fear that 'individuality and self-assertion and passionate feeling' will not simply be replaced by 'shrewdness and enterprise', but that the qualities which lead to rebellion and 'shrewdness' will be augmented by the technologies of modernity. Indeed, throughout his fiction and journalism written after the first two Home Rule bills, Stoker continually writes the fear that atavism is not something which decreases proportionately as modernity increases, but that the two nourish each other. Moreover, his attempts to disperse such a fear by entering it into writing only serve to perpetuate it. For instance, reporting on the Irish Exhibition held in Ballsbridge, Dublin, in 1907, Stoker makes an attempt to 'introduce Patrick to his new self' by contrasting the violent reputation of the Donnybrook Fair, on whose site the Exhibition has been erected, with the vision of modernity which the Exhibition promotes. 'The days of Donnybrook Fair and all it meant', he declares, 'the days of the stage Irishman and the stagey Irish play, of Fenianism and landlordism are rapidly passing away, if they have not even now come to an end' ('Great White Fair', 570-71). Rapidly passing away, perhaps – maybe even buried beneath the 'shining white' pavilions of the Exhibition of Irish industry, but the past is certainly not dead. Instead, the deeply disturbing recognition that 'Fenianism and landlordism' could exist in the same space as the typewriter, the telegraph and the railroad generates a series of texts at whose core is an anxiety that the 'natural' progress of civilisation is riddled with the unnatural survival of the past in the present.

IV

In a 1994 essay on the rhetoric of land and soil in nineteenth-century Ireland, Seamus Deane suggests in passing that we might read *Dracula* as the tale of an absentee landlord 'who is dependent in his London residence on the maintenance of a supply of soil in which he might coffin himself before the dawn comes' (33). 'Dracula's dwindling soil and his vampiric appetites', writes Deane, 'consort well enough with the image of the Irish landlord current in the nineteenth century' (34). While Deane does not develop this idea, it could be taken a step further. Not only is Dracula a landlord, he is a charismatic leader, so much so that the Catholic Slovaks and gypsies who follow him are prepared to die for him. In the writing of Ireland in the nineteenth century, from the time of O'Connell's Catholic Emancipation campaign in the 1820s to Matthew Arnold's lectures *On the Study of Celtic Literature* in the 1860s, the Catholic population of Ireland were similarly represented as vulnerable to the charms of a demagogue. 'The Celt', writes Arnold, is 'undisciplinable, anarchical, and turbulent by nature', but 'out of affection and admiration' gives himself 'body and soul to some leader'.

'That', he writes, 'is not a promising political temperament' (92-93). If O'Connell was such a leader in the 1820s and 1830s, in the 1890s the role could only have been filled by Parnell.

So, is Dracula Parnell? A landlord who is also a charismatic leader, intent on causing havoc in London, and driven by a fatal attraction to the bed of the wife of another man? More precisely, is he the Parnell of 1897, buried several years before but nonetheless unnervingly still alive in Irish political life?

However tempting such a positive identification might be, it might be more profitable to develop Deane's comments in another direction by looking at the importance of soil in Stoker's fiction. In particular, if we turn to his only novel set entirely in Ireland, *The Snake's Pass*,[8] we find that the soil of Ireland does indeed constitute a locus of anxiety. First published in serial form in *The People* in 1889, and in book form the following year, *The Snake's Pass* constitutes a point of intersection between the Irish concerns of Stoker's journalism and essays, and the displaced exoticism of his supernatural fiction. It is also the clearest instance of Stoker using the literary fantastic to write the condition of Ireland as unnatural.

The novel begins with Arthur, a young Englishman determined to improve his 'knowledge of Irish affairs by making a detour through some of the counties in the west' (13), finding himself in the vicinity of Croagh Patrick, regaled by the locals with legends of a moving bog. The bog of Shleenanaher – 'an that's Irish for the Shnake's Pass' – is unstable, constantly shifting and changing its form. 'Sure', says one of Stoker's peasant characters, 'they do say that the shiftin' bog wor the forrum the King of the Snakes tuk' to escape banishment when Saint Patrick drove the snakes from Ireland' (23). In addition, this shifting bog is reputed to be the hiding place of more than one lost treasure, including the golden crown of the mythical King of the Snakes, and a chest of gold coins left behind 'in the Frinch invasion that didn't come off undher Gineral Humbert' (24).

Having inscribed the bog in Irish folklore, a discursive power struggle ensues, in which the novel attempts to supplant this supernatural discourse with a natural explanation of the moving bog. On the morning after his introduction to the local legends of the area, Arthur meets an old friend, Dick Sutherland, 'who had gone into the Irish College of Science' (51). Dick is employed, albeit unwillingly, by the novel's villain, Black Murdock, to hunt for the treasure in the moving bog. In the early parts of the novel, the character of Dick allows Stoker room for long harangues concerning the shameful state of scientific investigation into Irish peatlands:

> You will hardly believe [says Dick] that although the subject [of
> bogs] is one of vital interest to thousands of persons in our own
> country – one in which national prosperity is mixed up to a large
> extent – one which touches deeply the happiness and material
> prosperity of a large section of Irish people, and so helps to
> mould their political action, there are hardly any works on the
> subject in existence (55).

As a statement of fact, this is not entirely accurate, for there was a
considerable literature on the bogs of Ireland in the nineteenth century. Stoker knew this, for his detailed accounts of the soil formations which produce the phenomena of the moving bog are taken,
almost verbatim, from Robert Kane's influential work of 1844, *The
Industrial Resources of Ireland*. Kane describes the way in which an
obstructed spring at the base of a bog can keep the soil in a 'rotten,
fluid state – the surface of the bog might be ultimately raised, and
its continuity below so totally destroyed, as to cause it to flow over
the retaining obstacle, and flood the adjacent country' (35).
Moreover, for Kane, the bogs of Ireland, in spite of their instability,
were a sign of the country's potential for industrial progress. 'Our
bogs may become', he writes, 'under the influence of an enlight-
ened energy, sources of industry and eminently productive' (32-33).
Nor was his opinion lost on entrepreneurs of the period, for as
Cormac Ó Gráda notes, 'the lack of success in developing peatbogs
for industrial use during the nineteenth century was not for want of
trying. The list of failures is an impressive one, spanning many
decades and many different processes' (323). Hence, Stoker is not
only factually incorrect in claiming that the bogs of Ireland lay outside of scientific discourse; his novel takes a subject which was ade-
quately explained by the laws of nature and juxtaposes it with
supernatural explanations. In so doing, he enters the soil of Ireland
into the uncertain realm of the literary fantastic.

Of course, Stoker was not the only person for whom the soil of
Ireland had been transformed into something unnatural in the late
1880s. Indeed, one might read this novel about the instability of
Irish land as a response to the 'Plan of Campaign', under which
thousands of tenant farmers throughout the country were refusing
to pay their rents as the novel was being published serially in 1889.
Here, however, we need to pause and resist the temptation to set up
Stoker as the favourite straw-man of Irish literary history, the
Ascendancy apologist with a bad conscience. Admittedly, as a
member of the Historical Society in 1872 Stoker had opposed

motions such as that of May 22, 'That England should prepare for an early Emancipation of her Colonies', and of June 19, 'That Mr Lecky is justified in his opinion that all Empires must eventually adopt Federalism as an alternative to dissolution' (*Address*, 57-58). However, Stoker's family were middle-class civil servants, not landowners, and by the time he wrote his *Personal Reminiscences of Henry Irving* in 1906, one of the heroes in a text prone to hero-worship is Gladstone, the prime mover of the Land Acts 1870 and 1881. Indeed, in the same text Stoker describes himself as 'a philosophical Home-Ruler' (29), and manuscript letters of his wife, Florence, suggest that during the 1890s the Stokers were friendly with John Dillon, an originator of the 'Plan of Campaign', and one of the most militant figures in the Irish Parliamentary Party in the late 1880s and 1890s.

What can we make of Stoker's relocation along the nationalist/imperialist political continuum? To begin with, it was not particularly unusual among urban middle class members of the Church of Ireland in the second half of the last century. One thinks, for instance, of Isaac Butt's evolution from young Tory to Home Ruler a generation earlier. In Stoker's case, what unites his youthful support for the Empire and later 'philosophical' endorsement of Irish Home Rule, is the attempt to construct a narrative of social progress which runs throughout his writing. In volume after volume in the first half of the nineteenth century, what is perceived as Ireland's low level of civilisation is attributed to the absence of large and prosperous middle class. When in the 1880s it became apparent that the consolidation of such a class depended upon the redistribution of land, Stoker's allegiances would appear to have undergone a shift. At the same time, however, the marked increase in agrarian violence which accompanied this change was understood, by those on all sides of the land debate, as unleashing the forces of a barbaric, repressed past. '"Why do you not forget the past?" say Englishmen over and over again to us', wrote R. B. O'Brien in *The Irish Land Question* of 1881. 'We answer, because you have never allowed us. By centuries of misrule you have kept alive its bitter memories'. 'It is impossible not to feel', he goes on to say, 'that there hangs over the country something like the shadow of the curse of past wrongs' (5).

That Stoker intended *The Snake's Pass* as an intervention in the Irish land debate of the late 1880s is clear. Indeed, shortly before the novel was launched on November 18, 1890, he sent a pre-publication copy to Gladstone, who, according to Stoker's *Reminiscences*, congratulated the author shortly thereafter on his presentation of 'a case of oppression by a "gombeen" man' (29).[9] Nor is it surprising that Gladstone would have identified the 'gombeen' man as the key to the novel, for the bifurcated vision of the Irish tenant farmer as both the embodiment of his nation's progress and as a violent, atavistic demon was frequently written in the late nineteenth century as two opposed character types: the 'peasant' and the 'gombeen man'. Such an opposition is present as early as 1847, for instance, in William Carleton's novel, *The Black Prophet*. We also find it a half century later when Lord Castletown of Ossory states that as part of 'A Definite Solution to the Irish Land Question', 'I want to protect from the gombeen man the peasant proprietors who have purchased their holdings' (Fitzpatrick, 130). In *The Snake's Pass*, Stoker participates in this discourse through the two contrasting characters who between them own the moving bog. One character, Phelim Joyce, is the virtuous Irish peasant to the point of caricature: honest, pious, plain-spoken, hard-working and father of an equally virtuous daughter. His counter-part, Black Murdock, the 'gombeen man', is the novel's villain, a 'black-jawed ruffian' (33) who curses, brawls, lies and cheats his way through the novel. Between them, they occupy the shifting ground of the moving bog, at one point even swapping their respective holdings.

When Black Murdock proposes marriage to Phelim Joyce's daughter, Nora, in a move which would unite their divided lands, the novel erupts into violence, unable to permit a resolution of these two conflicting images of the new Irish rural middle class, either on the level of narrative or on the level of the real. Faced with the impossibility of logical narrative closure, at the novel's end it is the actual soil of the bog which becomes the sign of ambivalence, as Black Murdock's digging into the bog causes it to become 'demoralised'. Once a heavy rain begins to flood down on the unstable earth, the whole bog begins to move, and in a final cataclysmic motion, the attempt with which the novel began to enter the bog into language collapses as the bog begins to slide down the hill. 'No language could describe the awful sensation of that melting away of the solid earth – the most dreadful nightmare would be almost a pleasant memory compared with it'. As it passes out of language, the bog loses its form: 'all things on its surface seemed to melt away and disappear, as though swallowed up' (228-29). This moment of dissolution is both the end and the apotheosis of the nineteenth-century liberal dream of a modern, progressive Ireland, as the soil – the focus of the most intense Irish political struggles in the 1880s – disappears into a shapeless, nameless mass.

Having swept down the side of the hill and into the sea, the bog swallows up Murdock and his house, leaving behind an empty landscape, a pastoral *tabula rasa*, on which the Englishman Arthur will eventually build a home with 'red tiled roof and quaint gables' (246). In this newly stable land left by the departing bog, the relics of Irish history – gold from the 1798 rebellion, a pre-Christian crown – are freed from their mythological power, and can be collected like so much booty. And yet, even in these final moments of the novel, when the work of science has apparently stripped the supernatural of its mystery, the fantastic is not entirely banished, as Dick and Arthur find an object not mentioned in the legends, nor predicted by their scientific investigations. Neither supernatural nor natural, carved into the rock which formed the bed of the shifting bog are 'inscriptions in strange character, formed by vertical lines something like the old telegraph signs, but placed differently', which Dick identifies as '"Ogham! – one of the oldest and least known of writings"' (241). In this curiously Lacanian moment, what began as a textual attempt to enter the bog into writing, and thereby decipher its secret, finds that language already exists in the heart of the bog; although this language resembles 'old telegraph signs' it is the language of the distant past, and it is unreadable.

* * *

A historicist reading of *The Snake's Pass* may appear to offer a measure of semantic stability; however, it by no means exhausts the text. As is the case in all of Stoker's other novels, the moment of cataclysm – whether the bog sliding down the mountain, the driving of a stake through Lucy's heart in *Dracula*,[10] the whirlwind which engulfs the final moments in *The Jewel of the Seven Stars*, or the storm in *The Watter's Mou* – has a sexual, orgasmic element, as the previously restrained hero and heroine come together in a moment of intense, obliterating union. Just as Franco Moretti has argued that *Dracula* will support both a Marxist reading and a psychoanalytical reading, so too would it be possible to read *The Snake's Pass* in both a historicist and a psychosexual way, even though there may not be any obvious link between the two. As Moretti points out, such texts 'wishing to incarnate Fear as such … must of necessity combine fears that have different causes: economic, ideological, psychical, sexual' (105). Identifying these causes, Moretti argues, requires a range of critical tools. And yet, in persistently reading Stoker as a British writer, critics (including Moretti, who argues that *Dracula* enacts a struggle between British nationalism and multinational capitalism (93)) have overlooked the possibilities for interpretation offered by colonial and post-colonial literary theory. Once we replace Stoker's text in an Irish frame, the element of the fantastic, that moment of unnatural anxiety which gives his texts their continuing power to disturb and invite interpretation, is recognised as what Homi Bhabha has called 'the colonial signifier – neither one nor other – […] an act of ambivalent signification, literally splitting the difference between the binary oppositions or polarities through which we think cultural difference' (128). Neither uncanny nor marvellous, neither natural nor supernatural, but like the bog in *The Snake's Pass*, 'ever under some uncomfortable or unnatural condition' (205), Stoker's writing has a place in that liminal space of the literary fantastic which may well be the characteristic structural form of colonial writing.

Notes

1. For a recent account of the continuing redefinition of Todorov's work on the fantastic, see Cornwell, *Literary Fantastic*, 11- 41.

2. The house is still standing today, a narrow, terraced three-storey dwelling near the centre of a gently curving row of similar late-Georgian houses built around a small park. In 1847, the park would have overlooked the tidal sloblands of Dublin Bay, now filled to make Fairview Park.

3. O'Grady, for instance, spoke six times during the 1871-2 academic year; Wilde and Carson joined in 1873-4, the year in which Stoker was ex-auditor.

4. See, for instance, Stevenson, 'A Vampire in the Mirror', 139-49.

5. Much has been made of the geographical siting of Dracula's homeland. Jean-Louis Shefer, for instance, equates it with complex theological debates over the nature of the eucharist in relation to the Byzantine Church. We might do well to remember, however, that Stoker's brother, George, served with the British army on Turkey's European border in the late 1870s, and his memoirs describe walking, Harker-like, 'among acres of dead and dying, feeling bewildered, and not knowing which way to turn, or where to begin' (x).

6. The *Shamrock* was owned and edited by Richard Pigott, who was

to commit suicide after being revealed as the forger of the Parnell letters in 1889. In one of the more unusual cases of life echoing art, Stoker published a conventional temperance tale in the *Shamrock* in 1875 entitled 'The Primrose Path'. It tells of an Irishman, Jerry O'Sullivan, who moves to London, is introduced to the demon drink, goes into a rapid decline, and commits suicide. The character who gives Jerry his first drink and leads him down the slippery slope is named Parnell.

7. Charlotte Stoker's account of a terrifying carriage ride through a deserted countryside to escape the cholera also suggests a point of intertextual reference for Jonathan Harker's carriage journey in the opening pages of *Dracula*. 'It was now raining as if heaven and earth were coming together', she writes, 'and after driving for about ten miles, my father looked very ill [...] We entered Donegal, but our arrival had been announced in some way and we found the square full of men howling like devils. In a trice ourselves and our luggage were taken, or rather torn from the carriage, the luggage was piled in the centre of the square, we placed on it, and a cry went out, "Fire to burn the cholera people!"' (Ludlam, 30).

8. Stoker's only other fictional work set entirely in Ireland is a very early tale, 'Buried Treasure', which appeared in the *Shamrock* in March of 1875.

9. Stoker sent Gladstone a pre-publication copy of *The Snake's Pass* during the second week of November, 1890. The novel was published on November 18, 1890, the same day as judgment was passed in the O'Shea divorce case, thereby signalling the beginning of the end of the alliance between Gladstone's Liberals and Parnell's Irish Parliamentary Party. Hence, it could be said that the novel appeared just as the debate in which it intervened was shifting its ground.

10. For a good account of the sexual drama of *Dracula*, see Craft, 'Kiss Me With Those Red Lips', 216-42.

Bibliography

Arnold, Matthew, *The Study of Celtic Literature* (1867), ed. A. Nutt, D. Nutt, London 1910.

Bhabha, Homi K., *The Location of Culture*, Routledge, London 1994.

Brooke-Rose, Christine, *A Rhetoric of the Unreal: Studies in Narrative and Structure, Especially of the Fantastic*, Cambridge UP, Cambridge 1981.

Conan Doyle, Arthur, *The Complete Sherlock Holmes Treasury*, Avenel, New York 1976.

Cornwell, Neil, *The Literary Fantastic: From Gothic to Postmodernism*, Harvester-Wheatsheaf, London 1990.

Craft, Christopher, '"Kiss Me With Those Red Lips": Gender and Inversion in Bram Stoker's Dracula', *Speaking of Gender*, ed. Elaine Showalter, Routledge, London 1989, 216-42.

Davitt, Michael, *The Fall of Feudalism in Ireland, or The Story of the Land League Revolution*, Harper, London 1904.

Deane, Seamus, 'Land and Soil: A Territorial Rhetoric', *History Ireland*, 2/1 (Spring 1994), 31-34.

De Vere, Aubrey, notebooks 1843-49, NLI MS 3747.

Farson, Daniel, *The Man Who Wrote Dracula: A Biography of Bram Stoker*, Michael Joseph, London 1975.

Fitzpatrick, Bernard E. B. (Lord Castletown of Upper Ossory), 'A Definite Solution of the Irish Land Question', *New Ireland Review* 5/3 (May 1896), 129-41.

Foucault, Michel, *The Order of Things: An Archeology of the Human Sciences* (1966), Vintage, New York 1994.

James, Henry, *The Aspern Papers and The Turn of the Screw* (1888; 1898), ed. Anthony Curtis, Penguin, Harmondsworth 1984.

'History of Ten Years', *Nation*, 8/46 (12 July 1847), 537.

Kane, Robert, *The Industrial Resources of Ireland*, Hodges and Smith, Dublin 1844.

Ludlam, Harry, *A Biography of Dracula: The Life Story of Bram Stoker*, Fireside, London 1962.

Malthus, Thomas Robert, *An Essay on the Principle of Population* (1798), ed. Anthony Flew, Penguin, Harmondsworth 1970.

Moretti, Franco, *Signs Taken for Wonders: Essays in the Sociology of Literary Forms*, revd. ed., transl. Susan Fischer, David Forgacs, and David Miller, Verso, New York 1988.

Newton, Isaac, *Mathematical Principles of Natural Philosophy*, ed. Florian Cajori, transl. Andrew Motte, University of California Press, Los Angeles 1934.

O'Brien, Richard Barry, *The Irish Land Question and English Public Opinion*, Sampson Low, Marston, Searle and Rivington, London 1881.

Ó Gráda, Cormac, *Ireland: A New Economic History 1780-1939*, Clarendon, Oxford 1994.

Pauperism: Is It the Effect of a Law of Nature, or of Human Laws and Customs Which are in Opposition, Effingham Wilson, London 1849.

'Priest-Hunting', *Nation*, 6/279 (5 Feb. 1848), 89.

Richards, Thomas, *The Imperial Archive: Knowledge and the Fantasy of Empire*, Verso, London 1993.

Schefer, Jean-Louis, 'The Bread and the Blood', transl. Stephen Bann, *Frankenstein, Creation and Monstrosity*, ed. Stephen Bann, Reaktion, London 1994.

Senior, Nassau W., *Journals, Conversations and Essays Relating to Ireland*, 2 vols., Longmans, Green and Co, London 1868.

Spencer, Herbert, *Essays: Scientific, Political and Speculative*, 3 vols., Longman, Green, Brown, Longmans and Roberts, London 1858.

Stevenson, John Allen, 'A Vampire in the Mirror: The Sexuality of Dracula', *PMLA* 103/2 (March 1988), 139-49.

Stoker, Bram, 'Buried Treasure', *Shamrock*, 12/439-40 (12-20 March 1875), 376-79, 403-06.

— 'The Censorship of Fiction', *Nineteenth Century and After*, 64/379 (Sept. 1908), 479-87.

— 'The Chain of Destiny', *Shamrock*, 12/446-9 (1-22 March 1875), 498-99, 514-16, 530-33, 546-48.

— *College Historical Society: Address Delivered in the Dining Hall of Trinity College at the First Meeting of the Twenty-Eighth Session on Wednesday Evening, November 13, 1872*, James Charles and Son, Dublin 1872.

— *Dracula*, (1897), ed. Maurice Hindle, Penguin, Harmondsworth 1993.

— *The Duties of Clerks of Petty Sessions in Ireland*, John Falconer, Dublin 1879.

— 'The Great White Fair in Dublin', *The World's Work* 9 (May 1907), 570-76.

— *The Jewel of the Seven Stars* (1903), Arrow: London 1962.

— *Personal Reminiscences of Henry Irving*, William Heinemann, London 1906.

— 'The Primrose Path', *Shamrock*, 12/434-38 (6 Feb.-6 March 1875), 289-93, 312-17, 330-34, 345-49, 360-65.

—*The Snake's Pass* (1890), Brandon, Dingle 1990.

— *Under the Sunset*, Sampson Low, Marston, Searle, and Rivington, London 1882.

— *The Watter's Mou*, Constable, London 1985.

Stoker, Florence, correspondence 1896, TCD MS 6872/59.

Stoker, George, *With the Unspeakables, or, Two Years Campaigning in European and Asiatic Turkey*, Chapman and Hall, London 1878.

Taylor, James, *Political Economy Illustrated by Sacred History*, Seeleys, London 1852.

Todorov, Tzvetan, *The Fantastic: A Structural Approach to a Literary Genre* (1970), transl. Richard Howards, Case Western Reserve, London 1973.

Tolkien, J. R. R., *The Hobbit, or, There and Back Again* (1937), Methuen, London 1976.

Vaughan, W. E., ed., *A New History of Ireland: Volume V: Ireland Under the Union, I, 1801-70*, Clarendon, Oxford 1989.

Wicke, Jennifer, 'Vampiric Typewriting: Dracula and its Media', *ELH* 59/2 (Summer 1992), 467-93.

Out of Nature:
Yeats's 'A Bronze Head'

Peter Denman

A Bronze Head

Here at right of the entrance this bronze head,
Human, superhuman, a bird's round eye,
Everything else withered and mummy-dead.
What great tomb-haunter sweeps the distant sky
(Something may linger there though all else die;)
And finds there nothing to make its terror less
Hysterica passio of its own emptiness?

No dark tomb-haunter once; her form all full
As though with magnanimity of light,
Yet a most gentle woman; who can tell
Which of her forms has shown her substance right?
Or maybe substance can be composite,
Profound McTaggart thought so, and in a breath
A mouthful held the extreme of life and death.

But even at the starting-post, all sleek and new,
I saw the wildness in her and I thought
A vision of terror that it must live through
Had shattered her soul. Propinquity had brought
Imagination to that pitch where it casts out
All that is not itself: I had grown wild
And wandered murmuring everywhere, 'My child, my child!'

Or else I thought her supernatural;
As though a sterner eye looked through her eye
On this foul world and its decline and fall;
On gangling stocks grown great, great stocks run dry,
Ancestral pearls all pitched into a sty,
Heroic reverie mocked by clown and knave,
And wondered what was left for massacre to save.

Yeats's involvement with the supernatural extends from his early sorties into nineteenth-century spiritualism to his later elaboration of the beliefs set forth in *A Vision*. The second and revised version of *A Vision*, published in 1937, probably represents the furthest extent of Yeats's engagement with a structure of belief and practice which informed his life and his poetry.[1] This essay examines how a sense of the supernatural, simply understood as signifying the possibility of reaching beyond nature, contributes to one of his final poems, 'A Bronze Head'. It is a difficult and discomforting poem, because its apocalyptic sentiments tend to express an almost antinomian disdain of this 'foul world' and its inhabitants.

'A Bronze Head' dates from the late 1930s, and it was published posthumously in March 1939. The eponymous bronze head is a bust of Maud Gonne, made by Laurence Campbell in plaster and painted bronze, and exhibited at the Municipal Gallery at Dublin. It shows a woman in her sixties, with strong sharp features and wearing a hat that fits close to the skull. Maud Gonne had been made to represent, for Yeats and for his readers, an image of beauty; here she is seen, for Campbell and herself, as an ageing woman full of fierceness and belonging more to history than to art. The virtue of a portrait, be it in a painting or a sculpture or a poem, is its fixity; it arrests time, or stands outside its imperatives – this is the conceit in Wilde's *Portrait of Dorian Gray* and the culmination of the Shakespearean sonnet's exultant 'So long as men can breathe, and eyes can see/ So long lives this, and this gives life to thee'. But the effect of the Campbell sculpture is suddenly to force a recognition that Maud Gonne has grown old; the conflict between the sculpted subject and the literary subject becomes a sign of flux and the restless onrush out of this life towards death.

The bust, like the woman it represents, is a material object with a tangible presence outside the poem. It is taken as the starting point for the poem and is mentioned twice in quick succession – in the title and in the opening line. The next two lines offer a descriptive commentary, but the tendency of the description is not to fix a clear image of the figure but to move away from it. The opening line, with its 'Here' and 'this', is strongly deictic, directing our attention to a specific location in the manner of a gallery guide. As we are supposedly being taken in to an art gallery, we are simultaneously ushered into the poem; the 'entrance' at the centre of the first line is also the entrance to the poem. It is all strikingly immediate, but soon the poem moves onto a very different level. 'Human, superhuman, a bird's round eye': in describing the head and in particular its eye(s), the line moves from the level of the human, which we all know and are comfortable with, to the superhuman: is this towards something approximating to the supernatural, or the Nietszchean superhuman?

It certainly transcends the merely human. And although the line lacks conjunctions or even paratactic links, the sequence invites us to read it as an ascending scale of intensity, not simply a set of alternatives. The bust looks human, with the shape of a woman's head, but it has about it the intensity of something more. The third term is 'a bird's eye', apparently a stage beyond even the superhuman. It is a puzzling progression, but Yeats himself has left some clarification in another poem. In the last stanza of 'Sailing to Byzantium' he imagines a progress out of the world:

> Once out of nature I shall never take
> My bodily form from any natural thing,
> But such a form as Grecian goldsmiths make
> Of hammered gold and gold enamelling
> To keep a drowsy emperer awake
> Or set upon a golden bough to sing...

The progress he imagines is away from humanity ('out of nature') to become a bird by way of a work of art. It is a metamorphosis suggested in other poems by Yeats. In 'Leda and the Swan', the helpless girl is imagined 'putting on the majesty and power' of her attacker. And 'Cuchulain Comforted' ends with the shades greeting the dead Cuchulain in the underworld, where 'They had changed their throats and had the throats of birds'.

While dwelling on the progress 'out of nature' enacted in 'A Bronze Head', it should be borne in mind that the bronze head represents Maud Gonne – or the subject she had become in Yeats's poems. In a very real way, therefore, the living person who has been transformed into an art image is here seen out of nature, as an art image. In the course of the poem, however, the bronze head is rapidly supplanted. By the end of the third line – perhaps even before then – this poem is no longer about the bronze head but about an idea of a living person.

The third line completes this first 'sentence' of the poem (it is not a sentence grammatically in that there is no main verb – the opening three lines function almost as a stage direction setting the scene for the rest of the poem). It tells of 'everything else withered and mummy-dead'. A distinction is drawn between the 'everything else' and some delimited object. That delimited object could be the head (and the woman it represents), with the world which she inhabits being the 'everything else' that is dead in contrast; or it could be the eye, in which case the dead 'everything else' might still have universal significance, or it might be pointing the contrast between the liveliness of the eye, and the face or body that is aged and dying. Again, if we refer to 'Sailing to Byzantium', there is the singing, clapping soul that inhabits the tattered coat upon a stick.

In the phrase 'mummy-dead', 'mummy' runs counter to the notion of death. The mummy is a supernatural image, in that it represents an effort to cross the threshold of mortality. It suggests a preserving, an expression of the desire to outlast the moment of death, and the belief that such transcendence is possible. 'Mummy' is a word or image that Yeats uses frequently in his later poems:

I need some mind that ...

                  can stay
Wound in mind's pondering
As mummies in mummy-cloth are wound.
('All Souls' Night')

For Hades' bobbin bound in mummy-cloth
May unwind the winding path.
 ('Byzantium')

    Those self-same hands perchance
...
Had scooped out Pharaoh's mummy.
('Vacillation')

The image quickly became part of Yeats's esoteric visionary system; in particular, the wrappings that wind around the mummified body served as a poetic image for the turning gyres.[2] Knowledge of mummies came directly from the contemporary newspaper headlines. The 1920s and 1930s had been the great age of the exploration of pyramids, most notably of Howard Carter's opening of the tomb of Tutankhamen. Reports on his findings were published from 1922 on, and came to exercise a hold on the popular imagination. Use of the mummy image in Yeats's poetry is found in *The Tower* and subsequent volumes, beginning with 'All Souls' Night' which dates from 1920 and was written to mark the completion of *A Vision*.

When 'tomb-haunter' is used in 'A Bronze Head' there is a shadowing also of Tutankhamen and the archaeological work on Egyptian tombs. The description is a further modulation of the bronze head/Maud Gonne figure, patrolling the sky like a spirit or supernatural being ('haunter'), frequenting places of death, but also like a bird in flight, searching with its eye. The images carry some supernatural import: the haunter from the after-life, and the bird which is 'out of nature', according to Yeats's own symbolic imagery. In the opening section of *A Vision*, words attributed to Michael Robartes had already linked birds with an anticipation of Armageddon and a violent cleansing:

> Dear predatory birds, prepare for war, prepare your children and all that you can reach, for how can a nation or a kindred without war become that 'bright particular star' of Shakespeare … Love war because of its horror, that belief may be changed, civilisation renewed. (52-53)

The other term, 'withered', is associated with decay, loss, and age. Yeats uses 'wither' in that relatively straightforward sense of deterioration in a number of poems: 'The Withering of the Boughs', 'The Rose Tree'. But it could also carry a different implication for him. There is a quatrain written some thirty years earlier called 'The Coming of Wisdom With Time' which turns on the use of 'withering' as a stripping down to vision and wisdom, and the entry into a higher state:

> Though leaves are many, the root is one;
> Through all the lying days of my youth
> I swayed my leaves and flowers in the sun;
> Now I may wither into the truth.

The passing away of life, freshness, and beauty brings compensatory access to a truth beyond nature.

'There' in the next line probably indicates the sky: the eye searches the sky hoping to find something that survives but (moving ahead to the last couplet of the stanza) it finds nothing. If we seek antecedents for the pronouns 'there' and 'its', 'there' must refer, in both instances, to the sky; but what about 'its'? This also could refer to the sky, but more probably to the *tomb-haunter – superhuman bird with a round eye – bronze head – 'Maud Gonne'* figure. The predominant emotion attributed to this composite figure is terror, which cannot be alleviated ('made less'); the terror is glossed as *'Hysterica passio'*, brought on by its own inner emptiness that is like the emptiness of the sky.

The first line of stanza two, 'No dark tomb-haunter once; her form all full', echoes aspects of stanza one. There is the repetition of the phrase 'tomb-haunter', again with a qualifying adjective – this time 'dark' rather than 'great'. The stanza's opening lines mirror the opening of the poem grammatically: again it is an elliptical phrase without a finite verb. With regard to the line-endings, there is a contrastive semantic link reaching across from the end of stanza one, 'emptiness', to the beginning of stanza two, 'full'. 'Emptiness' stands at the end of seven lines containing a thread of words and phrases such as 'Everything' 'Something' 'nothing': the 'everything' is 'everything else', exclusive rather than inclusive, a phrase echoed by 'all else' which might be added to this thread. All these somethings and nothings lead to 'emptiness', so that first stanza is characterised by absence. The second stanza is marked by presence, with an equivalent semantic thread of words such as 'full', 'substance' (twice), 'composite', and 'held'. This suggests a contrast between the predominating ideas of the two stanzas, borne out by the way stanza two begins: its opening phrase is one of forceful contrast, rewriting the descriptive terms of stanza one, where she was a 'great tomb-haunter' heading into the future; here we are told she was no tomb-haunter in the past. And now the *head-bird-tomb-haunter* figure becomes gendered for the first time, in the phrase 'her form all full'.

The language is beginning to respond to the theme of the poem. On the one hand there is a progress forward out of nature, towards non-humanity; on the other a harking back towards youthfulness and a 'most gentle woman'; the stanza's second line describes her full of 'magnanimity of light', where 'light' contrasts with 'dark' in the previous line. These are the two 'forms' under which she is imagined and presented, and the question arises as to which is the truer of the two: tomb-haunter or gentle woman? The movement out of these opposites towards a Hegelian synthesis brings the awkward introduction of McTaggart's name. Maybe substance can be a compound, a mix of the two opposites outlined in the first four lines; 'McTaggart thought so', and he also thought (a poetic illustration of the idea) that a breath contains within itself the uttermost of life and of death, or life and death seen as extremes opposed to each other. These opposite extremes have been given form in the images of the 'gentle woman' and 'tomb-haunter' respectively.

The third stanza describes the synthesis in the simultaneous presence of gentleness and wildness. It is a variation on an age-old trope in the lyric tradition about women loved and lost, as in Wyatt's 'They flee from me' with its rueful recollection that 'Once have I seen them gentle tame and meek/That now are wild'. In her eyes he saw the wildness which he explains by terror – surely akin to the terror mentioned at the end of stanza one. In the first stanza the terror is being lived through in the present; in the third stanza he recalls that somehow or other she anticipated that terror, as a destiny foreseen and a course to be endured. This pre-vision shatters her soul, notwithstanding the 'magnanimity of light', and it is apposite to bear in mind the etymology of 'magnanimity', with its meaning 'greatness of soul', or 'of spirit'.

Throughout this stanza the 'it/her' which hitherto has been the object of the poem is complemented by the introduction of the poet/speaker, in the first person. The pronoun 'it' is now released to signify 'imagination'; whose imagination is not specified, but from the context it must be the poet's own. In those early days, 'propinquity', or contact with her, affected him by casting out all else. In terms of their relationsip to each other, it describes an emotional obsession; in terms of the supernatural theme of the poem, it describes something more akin to possession.

It is at the end of this stanza that the poem becomes most self-centred, with the figure of the woman presented almost totally in terms of her relationship to the implied speaker. Furthermore, she is distanced from her human individuality in one of the several transformations that are enacted in the poem. It is 'about' (or it generates a version of) Maud Gonne; but she is originally present not as herself but as a sculpted simulacrum. The human qualities are brought into question; she is seen as a bird, then as gentle woman, then as a child. This progressive refusal to allow her her actual contemporary historical status as a sixty-year-old active public personality is counterpointed by the foregrounding of the poet himself. Practically elided from the first two stanzas, he now becomes overtly the channel for experience – 'I saw', 'I thought' – until at the end of this third stanza it is his words that are given in direct speech. She is progressively upstaged. At the opening of the poem the figure of the woman is pointed out and isolated; there ensues a closeness between her and the poet ('Propinquity'), which in turn is replaced by his predominance. He calls her 'my child'; it might be pointed out that Maud Gonne was just one year younger than Yeats, and outside the poetry his possession of her was in fact problematic. The repeated 'My child' is a term of affection; it may also be a sign of an attempt to fashion and hold a manageable image of the woman. The rhyme of 'wild' and 'child' is one of the most frequent in Yeats;[3] it is found in poems right back to 'The Stolen Child' at the beginning of his career, and subsequently in 'Owen Aherne', 'Towards Break of Day', 'Easter 1916' and 'Among School Children'.

Stanza four is a very rhetorical stanza, with the oratorically balanced phrases 'decline and fall', 'stocks ... dry', 'clown and knave'. It continues the construction of the composite. The 'Or else' which

introduces the next stanza is not so much a conjunction as an indication of an alternative way of thinking about her. Having outlined
one way – as a damaged fearful child – the poet now offers another
way, which in a composite being could possibly co-exist with the
child and not necessarily supplant it: she seemed to him to be
'supernatural'. The second line of this stanza takes us back to the
opening terms of the poem, with its repetition of the rhyme word
'eye' and a reprise of the progress away from the simplicity of the
merely human to the enhanced complexity of the superhuman. The
'sterner eye' invites the question `sterner than what?', and surely
suggests an eye that is sterner than the human one. This more-than-
human vision allows her to regard the world from a vantage point
that is beyond and outside the 'foul world' – looking down on it, literally and figuratively.

The poem pulls back to a survey – literally a bird's eye view – of
the moral condition of the world. It is a world of foulness, of family
stock deteriorating, and in a rewriting of the biblical proverb about
'casting pearls before swine' mixes concern for ancestral lineage
with the greasiness of the sty and the till. Yeats suggests a world in
chaos; no country for old men. Even the abstraction from the mundane that is 'Heroic reverie' cannot escape the mockery of the fool-
ish and the villainous; he had described the spiritual life in *A Vision*
at the highest level as being 'like that profound reverie of the somn-
ambulist which may be accompanied by a sensuous dream – a
Romanesque stream perhaps of bird and beast images – and yet
neither affect the dream nor be affected by it' (283). All the middle
lines of this stanza look at and comment on the world, and it ends
with speculation – a disinterested, detached wondering. Massacre,
avenging death, will be an agent of purification, but is there anything left to save, with 'save' here, I think, used in the sense of 'to
spare from the slaughter', or it could mean 'to redeem through the
act of massacre'. It is an unforgiving poem, apocalyptic, and one
that carries within it the uncomfortable tone of the elect, justified. A
sense of imminent massacre was readily felt in Europe at the time.

The bird becomes the vehicle and viewpoint for the poem, very
quickly displacing the bronze head. But is it possible to be more
specific about it? Yeats indicated that the bird he imagined in
'Sailing to Byzantium' was a golden artefact, but real birds figure
quite prominently in Yeats's poems. Often he names the type:
there's the single swan in 'Leda and the Swan', the fifty-nine wild
swans at Coole, the swallows – 'half a dozen in formation' – in
'Coole Park 1929', Juno's peacock, the phoenix, rooks of the 'rook-

delighting heaven'; the lake isle of Innisfree enjoys an 'evening full of linnets' wings'; later the falcon cannot hear the falconer, there is no hawk among his friends, there is a stare's nest by his window – the listing could go on, but once noticed, it is evident that Yeats could identify his birds if he so wished. After Yeats proposed to and was rejected by Maud Gonne in the 1890s, she remarked that she would like to be a seagull, if she were a bird; this prompted Yeats's poem 'The White Birds' in *The Rose*. So the conjunction of Maud Gonne and a bird had occurred before, and was indeed prompted by her. What about the bird in 'A Bronze Head'? It is not quite certain when the poem was written, but it was composed between 1937 and 1938. It is not clear whether it was started in 1937 and then left incomplete or worked at intermittently before being finished in 1938, or that it was written over a relatively brief period of time at some point in 1937 or 1938. The manuscript draft of the poem might indicate the latter; there's not a great deal of revision. *If* indeed it was the latter, and *if* the time it was written fell towards the end of the period bracketed by Mrs Yeats – i.e. mid- or late-1938 – then perhaps there is a link between this poem and a piece that Maud Gonne contributed to the Dublin monthly, *Ireland To-Day*, in March 1938. Invited to write its 'Letter of the Month', she sent in a vigorous but rather hectic essay on 'Fascism, Communism and Ireland' and the economic and financial domination of Ireland by Britain in the late 1930s, on the eve of the world war which she clearly foresees. She uses a striking image to characterise England, three or four times in the course of the letter – that of a vulture:

> Like a vulture hovering over battles to devour corpses, but without its savage innocence, England hovers over the battles she has prepared through her insensate claim to hold and dominate a third of the earth …

> England's inveterate worship of class and money should range her in the Fascist camp. But her middle-class fear its stern discipline as much as it fears Communism. The traditional policy of the vulture gives it greater scope; but today the vulture is hovering anxiously, …

> These points, common to Fascist and Communist Governments, are compatible with the Proclamation of the Republic drawn up in 1916 by a band of heroes of thought and act, and which was endorsed by the nation. They are not compatible with the Free State drawn on British lines, to permit the vulture to dig its claws into our flesh …

It is hard to resist the conjecture that this reference to the vulture might have attached itself to the idea of the author of the letter; after all, it is the bird that might be tomb-haunter, and attend at a massacre.[4]

Then there's that phrase 'tomb-haunter'. It has generally been glossed as referring to 'Maud Gonne MacBride's habit of attending funerals (on political occasions); she constantly wore long black flowing clothes and a veil in old age'. But there was one particular political funeral when she was sleek and new back in the 1890s, that of Parnell. Yeats did not go, fearing the press of the crowds would be too great, but Maud Gonne did:

> One of those near the grave had been the young girl, Maud Gonne, who according to one newspaper had travelled with the family in the first of the mourning-carriages. She was herself mourning the loss of a three-year-old daughter who had died only a few days before. She was a friend of the young poet W. B. Yeats, whom she told that evening in a state of some emotion that as Parnell was being buried a shooting star had suddenly appeared in the sky. The story of this portent, its significance undefined, went into legend. No other eyewitness of the burial at Glasnevin seems to have mentioned this, but it is an indisputable fact, recorded by the Dunsink Observatory, that at 6.30 p.m. that Sunday evening a remarkably brilliant bluish-white meteor 'much larger and brighter than Jupiter' was seen falling for four seconds in several parts of Ireland, 'lighting up the sky like a flash of lightning'.[5]

Yeats remembered this, and referred to it in his 1930s poem 'Parnell's Funeral':

> Under the Great Comedian's tomb the crowd.
> A bundle of tempestuous cloud is blown
> About the sky; where that is clear of cloud
> Brightness remains; a brighter star shoots down;
> ...
> But popular rage,
> *Hysterica passio* dragged this quarry down.
> None shared our guilt; nor did we play a part
> Upon a painted stage when we devoured his heart.

The star counteracts the emptiness of the sky, and – as if to reinforce a coincidental link with 'A Bronze Head' – there is the phrase 'Hysterica passio' as well. So, when the tomb-haunter is described as sweeping the distant sky and finding nothing but emptiness, perhaps we can conjecture what Yeats imagined her seeking. There had been signs and portents in her youth. The falling star is a portent familiar from folklore, and in Shakespeare's *Julius Caesar* .

The poem ends with a questioning, and while there is an appearance of closure it is in fact concerned with the search for a solution to a perceived problem. Its solution, 'massacre', is a terrible one. It arises as a consequence of the interchange between the natural and the supernatural domains. In effect, access to and a search of the supernatural may energise the individual but it does not proffer a recourse for mankind and the world in which we live.

The crux at the end rests in the ambiguity of the final lines. Who is wondering about the massacre? Is the grammatical subject of 'wondered' the 'sterner eye' looking through (and informing) the eye of the Maud Gonne figure, or is it the 'I' of the previous line, the poet's voice? The grammatical blurring enacts the propinquity of the two mentioned in stanza three, a propinquity further pointed by the homonymity of the two possible subjects, 'I' and 'eye'.[6] The pun facilitates an elision of the ethical subject at the centre of the poem, allowing the suggestion of terror to float free of any readily identifiable individual. The final phrase, in which the destruction of 'massacre' is presented as a means of salvation, does further violence to language. By the end of this relatively short poem, there has been considerable movement away from the bronze head which is its origin. It begins with the bronze head which represented, but was not, a human; it ends with a supernatural presence that operates above and outside the world of gentleness, continuity, and magnanimity. The recourse to the supernatural is essential to the poem's stance, allowing it to comment on the perceived decay of the world from a position of apparent disinterestedness. But the idea of the supernatural informs so many of the *Last Poems* of Yeats, and its use in 'A Bronze Head' can also be seen as a deeply personal stratagem as he looks back on a life lived in anticipation of release from nature.

Notes

1. Harper, *Yeats and the Occult*; Flannery, *Yeats and Magic*.

2. Ellman, *Identity of Yeats*, 157.

3. Perloff, *Rhyme and Meaning*.

4. Albright, in his notes to his edition of Yeats's *Poems*, suggests that the tomb-haunter seems 'an image of a raven or a vulture', on the basis of the 'bird's round eye' (832).

5. Kee, *Laurel and Ivy*, 12.

6. For some discussions of wordplay in literature, see Culler (ed.), *On Puns*.

Bibliography

Culler, Jonathan, ed., *On Puns: The Foundation of Letters*, Basil Blackwell, Oxford 1988.

Ellman, Richard, *The Identity of Yeats*, 2nd ed., Faber and Faber, London 1964.

Flannery, Mary Catherine, *Yeats and Magic: The Earlier Works*, Colin Smythe, Gerrards Cross 1977.

Harper, George Mills, ed., *Yeats and the Occult*, Macmillan, London 1975.

Kee, Robert, *The Laurel and the Ivy: The Story of Charles Stewart Parnell and Irish Nationalism*, Hamish Hamilton, London 1993.

Perloff, Marjorie, *Rhyme and Meaning in the Poetry of Yeats*, Mouton, The Hague 1970.

Yeats, W. B., *A Vision* (1937), Macmillan, London 1962.

— *The Variorum Edition of the Poems*, edited by Peter Allt and Russell K. Allspach, Macmillan, New York 1957.

—*The Poems*, edited by Daniel Albright, Everyman's Library, J. M. Dent and Sons, London 1992.

The Redeeming Vision:
Seamus Heaney's *Sweeney Astray*

Séamus MacGabhann

I

In Seamus Heaney's early work, culminating in *North*, the ancient feminine religion of Northern Europe had provided a lens which revealed the landscape to him as 'a memory, a piety, a loved mother' (*Preoccupations*, 141). Subsequently in *Sweeney Astray* and *Station Island*, the Christian religion of early Ireland, through the mythical tale of the suffering and displaced king Sweeney, furnishes the poet with a correspondingly powerful lens. It facilitates him in establishing a new mode of relationship with the Irish landscape, freeing his creative imagination from those restrictive obligations, religious, political and domestic, which he was constrained to adopt as part of what he terms 'that responsible adjudicating stance towards communal experience' (Randall, 18) typified by *North*. This stance, he now found, had bound him too closely to land and tribe.

In seizing upon the Sweeney myth, Heaney sees himself as akin to Thomas Kinsella who, in his translation of the *Táin* sagas and myths, finds 'an ordering structure for his own psychic materials and energies' (Deane, 70). Heaney is bent upon a similar undertaking to form his own psychic disposition into a kind of cultural landscape which could be stereoscopically viewed. He agrees with Seamus Deane that like Kinsella he too is 'obsessed with the desire that this landscape be distinctly of this culture' (Deane, 70), a notion he formed in writing the place-name poems, such as 'Anahorish', of *Wintering Out*. In writing those poems he had the joyful realisation that he could be faithful to the nature of the English language – 'for in some senses these poems are erotic mouth music by and out of the anglo-saxon tongue' (Deane, 70) – and at the same time remain faithful to his own non-English origin which for Heaney is County Derry. He tells Deane that it was in order to repeat this joyful experience of faithfulness to his own origin, of affirming his affinity with the land of south Derry and with the places of that part of Ulster that he began to translate *Buile Shuibhne*,[1] the medieval Irish tale of the sacral king, Sweeney, who is cursed by St Ronan, goes mad in battle and is driven out of Rasharkin, Co Antrim.

No more intimate approach to the land was possible than that available through the figure of Sweeney, for in early Irish tradition the sacral king was married to the land. Archaic pagan belief regarded the material Earth as a Mother. Fertility of this Earth Mother was sought 'when the ruler of the land was inaugurated with a ceremony which professed to espouse him to this divine mother, with the intent that his reign might be prosperous and that the earth might produce fruits in abundance' (O Rahilly, 21). In his espousal of his land the sacral king's inauguration ceremony was known as 'banais ríghi' or 'wedding-feast of kingship'.

II

At the commencement of *Sweeney Astray* (1983), Heaney's published version, Sweeney is an emblem of violence. As king of Dal nArie he is an aggressive warlord. He is a victor in single combat, a distinguished hero, duly rewarded by Congal Claon, his over-king, and mired in affection and territorial loyalty. When St Ronan encroaches upon his territory Sweeney attacks him ferociously and the cleric's curse precipitates his madness in battle and consequent overthrow.

Heaney, in his introduction to *Sweeney Astray*, sees the clash between Sweeney and St Ronan as exemplifying a 'tension between the newly dominant Christian ethos and the older recalcitrant Celtic temperament'. He points to 'the collision between the peremptory ecclesiastic and the sacral king, and ... the uneasy reconciliation set in St Moling's monastery' as 'explicit treatment of this recurrent theme'.

It is evident, however, that Sweeney's attack upon St Ronan need not be seen as the outcome of paganism alone. Outraged territorial piety in the face of St Ronan's intrusion upon his lands provides a clearer motive. Early Irish history furnishes many examples of raids by Christian kings upon monastic foundations. And rival monasteries themselves made war upon one another with recorded bloody consequences. Nor was there any specifically Christian-*versus*-pagan dimension to the historical battle of Magh Rath, fought in 637 AD, to which the Sweeney legend relates.[2]

The essential tension in the work is not that between Christian and pagan but rather that between the ascetic and the worldly. It is the tension between the ascetic ideal of the reformist monastic trad-

ition and, on the other hand, worldly secular life, including unre-
formed monastic life, from which Sweeney is exiled and banished
by St Ronan's curse.

The sacral king in early Irish society acted as a sort of lightning
conductor between his tribe and external forces and energies, spiritual and physical. Sweeney's outrage at St Ronan draws him into
conflict with a field of spiritual force so powerful that a major muta-
tion occurs in him. As medium between the spiritual and secular
worlds he is destined for transformation, rather than for any kind of
restoration. He is assimilated to the great current of spiritual energy
which fuelled the Céle Dé revival of the late eighth century.
Although the movement was never formalised and soon lost much
of its power, the ascetic ideal still retained power to command ven-
eration. 'In the tenth century and after the voyages were popularis-
ing the ascetic ideal as never before, lifting it out of the hard discipline of fact, into a world of adventure and enchantment' (Hughes,
Church, 177).

The nature of Sweeney's ascetic vision is established early in the
tale and we get a particularly powerful statement of it in the verses
in Section 23:

1. I perched for rest and imagined
   cuckoos calling across water,
   the Bann cuckoo calling sweeter
   than church bells that whinge and grind.

2. Friday is the wrong day, woman,
   for you to give birth to a son,
   the day when Mad Sweeney fasts
   for love of God, in penitence.

3. Do not just discount me. Listen.
   At Moira my tribe was beaten,
   beetled, heckled, hammered down,
   like flax being scutched by these women.

4. From the cliff of Lough Diolar
   to Derry Colmcille
   I saw the great swans, heard their calls
   sweetly rebuking wars and battles.

5. From lonely cliff-tops, the stag
   bells and makes the whole glen shake

and re-echo. I am ravished.
Unearthly sweetness shakes my breast.

6. O Christ, the loving and the sinless,
hear my prayer, attend, O Christ,
and let nothing separate us.
Blend me forever in your sweetness.

There is nothing recalcitrant, no deviant paganism evident here. The first verse contrasts the freedom of nature with the settled monastic life, to the disadvantage of the latter, a common theme in twelfth-century Irish literature. In verse two, the rebuke to the woman caught in the throes of childbirth has an ascetic severity which dramatically marks the distance Sweeney has moved from mundane reality. The most central human process – birth – is here seen as far inferior to Sweeney's fasting for love of God. Recalling in verse three the defeat of his tribe at Moira, he observes how as outcast in the natural world, he has been taught the vanity of human strife and discord. The great swans in their matchless beauty symbolise sweetness and harmony and so rebuke human discord and imperfection. The verse rises finally to the ardent outburst, Sweeney's prayer to the Christ with whom he has been united through his apprehension of the natural world. Christ's sweetness has been mediated to Sweeney through his experience of the natural world, God's creation. The pressing urgency of the last verse with its impassioned entreaty can be understood in terms of the threat which Sweeney feels from the immediacy of his former world. He has only begun to experience the surpassing sweetness of the natural world with Christ, a sweetness which he could lose forever. In these verses from *Sweeney Astray*, we can identify the isolated, highly personal and individual vision of Christ, conveyed in much hermit and nature poetry of the monastic tradition, particularly following upon the ascetic hermit or Céle Dé revival of the latter part of the eighth century.[3]

Sweeney's banishment and exile can be regarded as a version of pilgrimage, a practice common in the early Irish church in the pursuit of sanctity. As one historian notes:

A manuscript kept at Seir in the later Middle Ages was known as the 'Wanderings of Ciaran', a title which suggests the typical restlessness of the early Irish saint, constantly moving from place to place, reminding himself that here he had no continuing city. His journeys were not well-planned itineraries, determined in advance, he had no temporal destination; his aim was to live the ascetic life in exile, so he set out in pilgrimage for the Lord of the Elements, sometimes even entrusting himself to the seas without oars or rudder, like those Irishmen who came to land on the coasts of Cornwall in 891 'who had stolen away' says the Saxon chronicler, 'because they wished for the love of God to be on pilgrimage, they cared not whither'.

(Hughes, 'Irish Pilgrimage', 144)

In the same article, Hughes observes that St Columbanus in his eighth sermon, dealing with the essential instability and transitory nature of earthly life, speaks of our life as 'a roadway, where Christians must travel in perpetual pilgrimage as guests of the world (*hospites mundi*) content with a sort of travelling allowance'.

Part of the strategy of *Sweeney Astray* involves the development of Sweeney's dual response to the natural world – a response of terror and delight. In more general terms terror and delight are central to the early Irish Voyages or 'Immrama'. Sweeney's alienation may thus be viewed as an exotic version of such pilgrimage and exile. Even his growth of feathers is similar to the experience of saints in the Voyages.

Sweeney's role of penitent exile is thrust upon him. The process is one of purification and Sweeney endures with difficulty the privation and mortification which the anchorites sought actively. It is, however, through the welter of natural and supernatural forces in this crucible of suffering that he is purged of his former self and that his new spiritual identity is forged. In the end he is so assured in his new identity that he can meet the challenge of even so great a saint as Moling – and hold his own, as in Section 75:

Moling: And what knowledge has a fool
             about the hour of terce in Rome?
Sweeney: The Lord makes me His oracle
             from sunrise till sun's going down.
Moling: My ministry is only toil
             the weak and strong both exhaust me.
Sweeney: I toil to a bed on the chill
             steeps of Benevenagh.

He further explains to Moling that his own affliction is that God denies him repose on earth. The conclusion of his arduous pilgrimage cannot be among mortal men. The true home of his spiritual being is elsewhere:

Sweeney: The resting place that I prefer
             is life in everlasting peace.

The metamorphosis of Sweeney, the aggressive warlord, can thus be seen as a version of the drama of Christian redemption. Sweeney's pilgrimage of expiation involves acute suffering for his violence. That suffering is made the vehicle for the development of an intensely realised spiritual vision, expressed in what Heaney describes in his introduction as a 'primer of lyric genres – laments, dialogues, rhapsodies, curses'. The outcast Sweeney's strikingly realised spiritual vision constitutes a radical critique of the pugnacious values which he had embodied in his office of sacral king. It is a critique also of the establishment values of worldly monastic and secular life.

III

Sweeney's radical transformation is eminently amenable to Heaney's artistic purpose. Just as the poet had appropriated for purposes of his art the archaic victims of the violent cult of Nerthus, so he appropriates here the pilgrim-victim Sweeney, whom he describes in the introduction as 'a figure of the artist, displaced, guilty, assuaging himself by his utterance', so that the work can be read as a version 'of the quarrel between free creative imagination and the constraints of religious, political and domestic obligation'. Heaney realises that Sweeney can become a vehicle by which he may flee from such obligation, facilitating thereby the development of his own artistic vision. Sweeney's rebirth as a visionary poet has especial significance for Heaney. His 1972 translation of *Buile Shuibhne* represented a rebirth for the poet.[4] He had arrived in Glanmore in Wicklow, in flight from the immediacy of the Ulster troubles. The translation was no neutral commission but was rather 'a way of housing things that I had in me anyway' (O'Toole), having some inward connection with the work he was doing at the time:

> At that time what was happening to me in Wicklow, I think, was a kind of retrieval of the first life that I had in the countryside. I mean things as simple as seeing a bush budding, leaves coming up. Of course you saw them before, but living right at the window level with briars and vegetation and stones, mossy stones, on those gates, it was as if the eye-level of a child was reanimated and it seemed to me that Sweeney in the branches could conduct a lot of that energy out of me into words. That was my notion, that was my excitement. (O'Toole)

The version which resulted (as found in the 1972 National Library MS) was a highly lyrical, very lush verse where the poet takes considerable liberties with the original. For instance, the royal garb of the proud warlord, Sweeney, before the battle of Moira, is described, in part, as follows:

> next his white skin, the kisses of silk;
> his girdle, a satin embrace;
> his tunic, his valour's insignia,
> a reward of service, a clasp of friendship from Conall (*sic*).

In the published version this description is rendered in a plainer, stricter idiom:

> next his white skin, the shimmer of silk;
> and his satin girdle around him;
> and his tunic, that reward of service
> and gift of fealty from Congal. (Section 8)

Heaney's concern with contemporary political strife in Ulster also infiltrates the idiom of the first version. Nationalists were currently accusing Unionists in Northern Ireland of 'bully boy tactics' and St Ronan is accorded this idiom as he deplores Sweeney's outrage upon him:

> My relief
> was a pivot of history.
> A snap of Donal's fingers
> called off the bullyboy.

The published work remains closer to the original and conveys this more accurately as follows:

> So I offered thanks and praise
> for the merciful release,
> that unhoped-for, timely summons
> to arm and join the high prince. (Section 6)

Towards the end of the 1972 version, Heaney's tendency to wrest the original to his purpose was modified and the work became what he describes as 'artistically broken-backed' (O'Toole). He was unhappy with the result and put the manuscript away for seven years. By the time of his return to it at the end of the seventies the softness and lushness of language had been tempered. He now had a distrust of lyric sweetness and had formulated a notion in the meantime that

> the right noise for Sweeney would be the clear hard line, a cold temperature and a very bare style. That could be the ideal that would never be realised, that kind of steel pen chill in the writing. It was a very deliberate enterprise in taking away the sweet-

ness and making it more literal and more faithful to the content
of the Irish. (O'Toole)

Consideration of a short excerpt from the work, the verses of
Section 73, clearly illustrates Heaney's point. The original Irish of
Buile Shuibhne reads:

All Fharannáin, adhbha náomh,
Co n-iomad call caomh is cnúas,
uisge tinnesnach can tess
ag snige re a chness anúas.

As iomdha ann eidhnech ghlass
agus meass re mberar geall
agus abhall chenntrom chaomh
ag filliudh a chraobh fa cheann.

Imdha broc ag dol fa a dhíon,
ann is míol muighe nach mall,
is édan rionntanach róin
ag techt ón muir móir anall.

Mé Suibhne mac Colmáin chóir,
mór n-oidhchi reíidh bhím co fann,
romthruaill Rónán do Druim Gess,
codlaim fa chraoibh 'san ess tall.

In the 1972 version these verses are rendered thus:

The tabernacle of the hazel wood
on the cliff at Farannan
and the cataract glittering
like the stem of a chalice!

Here's a green miracle
of oak-mast and ivy,
where the loaded branch
bends over windfalls.

Badgers earthing in the banks
hares in the grass
and the seals' heads
cobbling the swell.

You'll find me under a tree
by the waterfall,
a riddled oak-apple
wintered and gnawed at.

In their published form in *Sweeney Astray* these verses are modified
as follows:

Sainted cliff at Alternan
nut grove, hazel-wood!
Cold quick sweeps of water
fall down the cliff-side.

Ivies green and thicken there,
its oak-mast is precious.
Fruited branches nod and bend
from heavy-headed apple trees.

Badgers make their setts there
and swift hares have their form;
and seals' heads swim the ocean,
cobbling the running foam.

And by the waterfall, Colman's son,
haggard, spent, frost-bitten Sweeney,
Ronan of Drumgesh's victim,
is sleeping at the foot of a tree.

The strategy of Heaney's 1972 version is to allow the original to suggest images. Thus the hazel wood is a 'tabernacle', the abundant greenery is 'a green miracle', and Sweeney is represented figuratively as 'a riddled oak-apple'. The images give leverage to the imagination and the verse takes off from there. Clearly such imaginative levitation can loft the poetry to a considerable distance from the original. The concrete directness of the Irish has a chastened particularity which Heaney fails to catch. His relish of lushness and the exaggeration of the sacramental, in terms like 'tabernacle', 'chalice' and 'miracle', are a violation of the elemental discipline of the Irish.

These effects of relish and exaggeration are toned down and muted in the *Sweeney Astray* version. Now he moves closer to the Irish and this fidelity to the original gives a definiteness, a harder edge and a cooler temperature to the verse. In 'The God in the Tree' in *Preoccupations* Heaney had praised Flann O'Brien's accurate notation of 'the steel-pen exactness' of medieval Irish lyric. Now he aspires towards that clarity and cleanliness, and the lines of the published version have a brightness and exactness approximating more closely to the precision of the Irish.

Both of Heaney's versions demonstrate the poet's intimacy with the natural world, corresponding to an aspect of his retrieval in Glanmore of his first life in the countryside. Names of places are now to be savoured and celebrated. Place is to be known through its flora and, as in the following example, through its fauna:

> The stag of high Slieve Felim,
> the stag of the steep Fews,
> the stag of Duhallow, the stag of Orrery
> the fierce stag of Killarney.
>
> The stag of Islandmagee, Larne's stag,
> the stag of Moylinny,
> the stag of Cooley, the stag of Cunghill,
> the stag of the two-peaked Burren. (Section 40)

By means of a whole range of lyric strategies, laments, dialogues, litanies, rhapsodies, curses, an extraordinarily comprehensive evocation of the landscape of Ireland is presented through the intimate natural life of such places. Heaney conveys the spirit and word music of the original very effectively with further 'erotic mouth music by and out of the saxon tongue', while once more being faithful to his own non-English origin. For example, the heartbroken Sweeney laments his lot as follows in *Sweeney Astray*, Section 45:

> the sough of the winter night,
> my feet packing the hailstones
> as I pad the dappled
> banks of Mourne
>
> or lie, unslept, in a wet bed
> on the hills by Lough Erne,
> tensed for first light
> and an early start.
>
> Skimming the waves
> at Dunseverick
> listening to billows
> at Dun Rodairce.

In such naming of place as this, he conjures up the secret identity of his region and his country, a revelation effected through Sweeney's purified perception. A central aspect of Sweeney's altered vision is the change in his attitude to place. His reign as sacral king ends with his headlong flight from the battle of Moira as a result of St Ronan's curse. Henceforth, home for Sweeney becomes the landscape of the whole of Ireland and a part of western Scotland. As dispossessed outcast, Sweeney has no more claim than a transient bird of the air upon any part of that landscape. Now his purified, alienated vision incorporates a rich dimension of the ascetic hermit poetry of the early Irish church, and conveys a striking sense of the pristine beauty and sensuous immediacy of the landscape, sharpened by a

growing awareness of it as God's creation. His former narrow and
ferocious possessiveness of place is ousted by a complex of atti-
tudes ranging from lament to celebration, so that the topography of
Ireland, considered in its totality, becomes lyrically alive in his
utterance.

This concern with place and placenames relates *Buile Shuibhne* to
the Irish tradition of 'dindshenchas'. The word 'dind' means a noteworthy place, and 'dindshenchas' is the tradition relating to such
places, recording in particular how they got their names. As Máirín
O'Daly observes: 'The Dindshenchas deals not only with dwelling-
places, battlefields and places of assembly, but also with purely natural features, mountains, rivers, lakes, for the material of the tales
draws very little upon history and to a great extent upon mythology' (O'Daly, 59). Hence the Dindshenchas was the body of lore
which since earliest times linked people to place in Ireland and this
would have included giving historical ratification to territorial
claims.

Seamus Heaney is much concerned with this aspect of place in
Sweeney Astray. In his introduction he says: 'My fundamental relation with Sweeney, however, is topographical. His kingdom lay in
what is now south County Antrim and north County Down, and
for over thirty years I lived on the verges of that territory, in sight of
some of Sweeney's places and in earshot of others, Slemish,
Rasharkin, Benevenagh, Dunseverick, the Bann, the Roe, the
Mournes'. Heaney then wishes once more to cross his lived experience in these places with the dimension available now from his
erudition. For him, the Irish text becomes a key to unlock the identity
of place. He was, in addition, determined that the tale in translation
should be accessible and available to Unionists in the North who
reject the Irish tradition and do not see themselves as part of it. Of
central importance here was the matter of the placenames which
appear in the text:

> I decided as far as I could to translate the place-names into their
> modern equivalents. One of the functions that I saw for the thing
> was that it should give some kind of common possession. That
> was my 1972 notion and I think I still have it. I think that work
> which binds people to the ground, to the place where they are, is
> a service of some sort. And that work should belong to the peo-
> ple of Moira and Antrim and Dunseverick, which are mentioned
> in the text. It was important that Dunseverick wouldn't be *Dun
> Samhairce* or Moira be *Magh Rath*. (O'Toole)

By using the anglicised names by which these Ulster places are known today, Seamus Heaney gives the contemporary landscape a new dimension. He bequeaths to the people there the possibility of a renewed vision, of a life-enhancing and liberating perception of themselves, a vision of true fertility, plenitude and peace. The poet emphasises in his introduction that it is possible

> to dwell upon Sweeney's easy sense of cultural affinity with both western Scotland and southern Ireland as exemplary for all men and women in contemporary Ulster, or to ponder the thought that this Irish invention may well have been a development of a British original, vestigially present in the tale of the madman called Alan.[5]

IV

In *Sweeney Astray* the places and landscape of present-day Northern Ireland are liberated into a context that is mythical and mystical. The actuality of these places is tempered; their hermetic, obdurate, oppressive, contemporary nature is rendered more plastic and they are infused with an identity which resonates beyond present limitation. Clearly this also entails the transcendence of obdurate political limitation. Political, sectarian actuality is rendered less oppressively compelling. Since the myth is independent of the laws of nature, it can penetrate and transcend the bounds of the temporal and material world. Hence the Christian myth of Sweeney yields a paradigm of a politics of true detachment, a politics ultimately of profound liberation. Such liberation is akin to that offered by Eliot in 'Little Gidding'. Here Eliot's *persona* 'constitutes a proof – sufficient for the imagination, at least – that an ordained and suprahistorical reality persists' (Heaney, *Government of the Tongue*, 43). Contemplating purgatorial renewal through the refining fire 'Where you must move in measure, like a dancer', the speaker affords us the consolations of the visionary perspective:

> This is the use of memory:
> For liberation – not less of love but expanding
> Of love beyond desire, and so liberation
> From the future as well as the past. Thus, love of a country
> Begins as attachment to our own field of action
> And comes to find that action of little importance
> Though never indifferent. History may be servitude,
> History may be freedom. See, now they vanish,
> The faces and places, with the self which, as it could, loved them,
> To become renewed, transfigured, in another pattern.

This is the use of memory for Heaney also. His deployment of the Sweeney myth facilitates such an awakening from the nightmare of history. Drawing upon Celtic imagination and racial memory, he uses the Sweeney vehicle to penetrate the oppressive past more profoundly, throwing into fresh relief the excesses of attachment. Through this 'expanding of love' we move as it were into a different dimension of being, from material to spiritual, from outer to inner space. Our perceptions of the universe and of our place in it are powerfully questioned. Memory, through the medium of the Sweeney myth, allows Heaney to distil from the past new patterns which have the power to renew and transfigure the circumstances of our lives, tempering the rigidity of time and offering release from the servitude of excess. What emerges finally in the redeeming vision of *Sweeney Astray* is an amplified sense of place and an augmented sense of possibility, in effect a country of the mind which profoundly challenges our generosity of response.

Notes:

1. O'Keeffe, ed., *Buile Shuibhne*: see Bibliography. Seamus Heaney's published version, *Sweeney Astray*, 1983, omits parts of the linking prose narrative of the original which frequently anticipates or repeats the verse content. In addition, Heaney states that 'six stanzas have been dropped from Section 16, seven from Section 40 and one from Section 43-Section 82 and the first fifteen stanzas of Section 83 have also been excluded', 'Notes and Acknowledgements', *Sweeney Astray*. Ciaran Carson observes that four consecutive stanzas in Section 45 have been omitted without acknowledgement. See 'Sweeney Astray', 143. To this I would further add that one stanza from Section 43 and one stanza from Section 58 have also been omitted without indication.

2. For historical background to the battle of Magh Rath see Byrne, 112-14. See also Charles-Edwards and Kelly, *Bechbretha*.

3. O'Dwyer, gives a detailed account.

4. Seamus Heaney presented the manuscript of his unpublished 1972 version of *Buile Shuibhne* to the National Library of Ireland in November 1986. I am grateful to the poet and to the National Library for permission to examine this material.

5. Jackson holds that the tale of the Wild Man originated in Dál Riada, the Irish kingdom in Scotland. Carney argues for an origin in the British kingdom of Strathclyde. Both scholars give an impres-

sive insight into the evolutionary development of the tale and explain how the Suibhne and Moling association arises. Lehmann, through detailed analysis of textual evidence, also demonstrates the evolutionary nature of the story. Ó Riain studies how the tale was given final shape in the twelfth century with the propagandist addition of the Ronan episode in its present form. Cohen provides further valuable insights into the complex evolutionary nature of this work through his application of the theories of Dumézil on Indo-European mythology.

Bibliography

Byrne, Francis John, *Irish Kings and High-Kings*, Batsford, London 1973 and 1987.

Carney, James, '"Suibhne Geilt" and "The Children of Lir"', *Éigse* VI (1950), 83-110.

Carson, Ciaran, 'Sweeney Astray: Escaping from Limbo', in Tony Curtis, ed., *The Art of Seamus Heaney*, Poetry Wales Press, Bridgend 1985, 141-48.

Charles-Edwards, Thomas and Fergus Kelly, eds., *Bechbretha: an Old Irish law-tract on beekeeping*, Institute of Advanced Studies, Dublin 1983.

Cohen, David, 'Suibhne Geilt', *Celtica* XII (1977), 113-24.

Deane, Seamus, 'Unhappy and at Home: Interview with Seamus Heaney', *The Crane Bag* 1/1 (1977), 61-67. Reprinted in M.P. Hederman and R. Kearney, eds., *The Cranebag Book of Irish Studies 1977-1981*, Blackwater Press, Dublin 1982, 66-72.

Heaney, Seamus, *Preoccupations: Selected Prose 1968-1978*, Faber and Faber, London and Boston 1980.

— 'Sweeney Astray', 1972 unpublished manuscript, the National Library of Ireland.

— *Sweeney Astray*, Field Day Theatre Company, Derry 1983 and Faber and Faber, London 1984.

— *The Government of the Tongue*, Faber and Faber, London and Boston 1988.

Hughes, Kathleen, 'The Changing Theory and Practice of Irish Pilgrimage', *Journal of Irish Ecclesiastical History* XI (1960), 143-51.

Hughes, Kathleen, *The Church in Early Irish Society*, Methuen, London 1966.

Jackson, Kenneth, 'The Motive of the Threefold Death in the Story of Suibhne Geilt', in Rev. John Ryan, ed., *Féilscríbhinn Eoin Mhic Néill*, Dublin 1940, 535-50.

Lehmann, Ruth P., 'A Study of the Buile Shuibhne', *Études Celtiques* VI (1953-1954), 289-311 and VII (1955-1956), 115-38.

O Daly, Máirín, 'The Metrical Dindshenchas', in James Carney, ed., *Early Irish Poetry*, Mercier Press, Cork 1965, 59-72.

O Dwyer, Peter, *Céle Dé*, Carmelite Publications, Dublin 1981.

O'Keeffe, J.G., ed., *Buile Shuibhne, with an English translation*, Irish Texts Society, vol.XII, Dublin 1913.

O'Rahilly, T.F., 'On the Origin of the Names Érainn and Ériu', *Ériu* XIV (1946), 7-28.

Ó Riain, Pádraig, 'The Materials and Provenance of Buile Shuibhne', *Éigse* XV (1974), 173-88.

O'Toole, Fintan, 'Heaney's Sweeney', *The Sunday Tribune*, November 20, 1983, 12.

Randall, James, 'An Interview with Seamus Heaney', *Ploughshares* 5/3 (1979), 7-22.

Into Which West?:
Irish Modernity and the Maternal Supernatural

Joe Cleary

The prime cause of the retreat from enlightenment into mythology is not to be sought so much in nationalist, pagan and other modern mythologies manufactured precisely in order to contrive such a reversal, but in the Enlightenment itself when paralyzed by fear of the truth.

— Theodor Adorno and Max Horkheimer, *Dialectic of Enlightenment*

I

Cinema in Ireland is usually said to begin in Dublin on 20 April 1896 with the first public screenings of films in Dan Lowrey's *Star of Erin Theatre of Varieties* (now the *Olympia*). The establishment of moments of origin is always a precarious business, however, and it might be argued that, at the level of discourse at least, cinematography had already made a significant and controversial appearance in Ireland some seventeen years earlier, not in Dublin but at the site of Ireland's most famous manifestation of the supernatural in modern times: that is, in the small rural village of Knock, County Mayo, where on the night of 21 August 1879 fifteen people claimed to have witnessed an apparition of the Blessed Virgin against the outside gable wall of the local parish church. For those sceptical about the authenticity of this apparition, cinematographic projection provided a means to rationalise the inexplicable, to demystify the apparently supernatural. The sceptics argued that even if the fraudulent collusion of the witnesses was ruled out, the apparition could still be explained by natural means. The witnesses, it was suggested, were themselves the victims of an ocular delusion achieved either by projecting an image of the Blessed Virgin onto the gable wall of the church using some sort of magic lantern or, alternatively, by painting the figure onto the wall of the church with some phosphorescent substance which might later have been illuminated with a magnesium lamp.

The hypothesis that the Marian apparition was really the work

147

of a hidden projectionist is one which would seem to place cinematography in this instance firmly on the side of a materialist
rationalism. Cinematography, that is to say, figures within the
hypothesis as yet another instrument in the arsenal of what Weber
described as the rationalist disenchantment of the world. Things
are not quite so clear-cut as this suggests however. After all, the
hypothesis that the apparition might naturally be accounted for as
an ocular delusion produced by a hidden projectionist was first
advanced not by some anti-clerical rationalist but by a Dr Francis
Lennon, himself a member of the clergy and a Professor of Natural
Philosophy at St Patrick's College, Maynooth. Dr Lennon advanced
this theory in his report to Archbishop Cavanagh who had asked
him to investigate the circumstances of the apparition shortly after
it had occurred. What we find here, then, is not a simple polar
opposition between religious irrationalism and materialist rationalism, but a more complex event in which the Catholic Church finds
itself in the awkward position of having to negotiate some form of
accommodation between the scientific standards of a modern
worldview and a belief in the miraculous inherent in its own doctrines. Moreover, the argument that the apparition was only a
'trick' of the camera is one freighted with the clear if unspoken
inference that cinematography itself belongs intrinsically to the category of the fraudulent: cinematography, in other words, not as an
instrument of demystification, but as a technology of mystification
– one capable in fact of simulating its own 'false' or 'degraded' version of the experience of the miraculous.[1] What had seemed initially,
then, to be a rather straightforward opposition between cinematography and the church, with the one unambiguously on the side of
modernity and the other unambiguously resistant to it, proves on
closer inspection to be an event in which neither church nor cinematography seems quite so clearly positioned on the side of
enlightenment.[2]

For the sociologist of religion, the remarkable proliferation of
Marian apparitions in nineteenth century Europe – at least nine
major apparitions occur in the period between 1830 and 1933; five
in France, two in Belgium, one each in Portugal and Ireland – is
generally considered in the context of the long struggle between
religious and Enlightenment conceptions of the world, a struggle
waged with great intensity throughout this entire period.[3] At a time
when a secular rationalist outlook was increasingly becoming the
intellectual dominant, popular Catholic acceptance of the Marian
apparitions argued a continuing belief in the supernatural which

ran directly counter to the prevailing intellectual climate. The establishment of 'supernaturalist' doctrines as dogmas of Catholicism, such as the Immaculate Conception in 1854, can be seen as gestures on the part of the church authorities which lent ecclesiastical support to this defiance of the prevailing rationalist *Weltanschauung* (Warner 1985, 236-37).

In the latter half of the nineteenth century, however, Roman Catholicism was not the only area in which the figure of what might be termed the 'Great Mother' would become an issue of considerable importance. In 1861 Johann Jacob Bachofen, a Swiss-German student of philosophy and ancient law, published his work *Das Mutterrecht* which first proposed the idea that the original form of human social organisation was the matriarchal clan, an arrangement emanating from the more obvious reproductive role of the female. In *Das Mutterrecht*, Bachofen argued not only for the historical priority of maternal over paternal kinship, but also that the matriarchate constituted an epoch in human history when women were powerful and influential, remaining so until a patriarchal revolt reversed the balance of power between the sexes. Bachofen's work clearly belongs to the world of nineteenth century romantic idealism, but the idea of the matriarchate would eventually find its way into socialist thought by way of Frederick Engels' *The Origin of the Family, Private Property and the State* (1891). Although critical of what he held to be Bachofen's idealist treatment of mother-right, and leaning more heavily on the work of ethnologist Henry Lewis Morgan, whom he believed to have put the subject onto a more solidly materialist footing, Engels accepted the notion of the matriarchate as a general phase in human history, one which was only overthrown by patriarchy when human society was on the threshold of the development of privately owned wealth and the formation of class society.[4] Twentieth century anthropology would generally come to reject the idea of the matriarchate and relegate it to the status of a curiosity in the history of the discipline. The matriarchate retained a certain currency both in Soviet anthropology and in Western popular culture, however, long after it had been rejected in Euro-American academic anthropology. In certain forms of feminism and in some strands of the ecological movement in the West, the idea of the matriarchate has even come to enjoy something of a late twentieth century resurgence (Fluehr-Lobban, 1979).

What interests me in all of this is the way in which the figure of the 'Great Mother' seems to acquire a certain prominence from the latter half of the nineteenth century onwards in a whole variety of very different discourses: religious, romantic, socialistic, feminist, and even ecological. Clearly, the 'Great Mother' does not mean the same thing in all of these different discourses. Yet, setting aside for the moment their mutual antipathy to each other, what these different discourses do appear to share in common is a certain dissatisfaction with modernity, and in each case the deployment of the figure of the 'Great Mother' would seem to be pivotal to the expression of this dissatisfaction. Whether it takes the secular form of some matriarchal epoch before the advent of capitalism and/or patriarchy, or the religious form of Marian apparitions mourning or admonishing the 'sins' and 'excesses' of modernity (with socialism often held to be the chief of these), or feminist attempts to recover a female deity, the figure of the 'Great Mother' operates in all of these different modalities as the sign of a utopian desire for some alternative to the world as it presently exists.[5]

Viewed against this wider historical and intellectual context, the events in Knock in 1879 begin to seem less 'provincial', less the product of Irish 'exceptionalism', perhaps, than they are sometimes assumed to be. Moreover, the issues provoked by those events continue to resonate in our contemporary moment as well. In 1985 Ireland was swept by a veritable wave of Marian apparitions all the way from Ballinspittle in County Cork to Carns in West Sligo. That people thronged in their thousands to witness these apparitions was acknowledged by all at the time to be a sign of a deep cultural malaise, though opinions differed widely as to the exact source of that malaise. If Irish fascination with the figure of the 'Great Mother' was restricted to these apparitions, it would be easy to conceive of the phenomenon as an exclusively Catholic affair, and to think of it as something essentially marginal to the preoccupations of modern secular Ireland. There is good reason to question this assumption, however, since the haunting figure of the 'Great Mother' continues to make its presence felt in the ostensibly secularised world of Irish mass culture as well. In 1991 Dermot Bolger's play, *One Last White Horse*, was performed in the Peacock Theatre. Set in Dublin, Bolger's play is centred around a male heroin-addict, Eddie, who has recurrent hallucinations of a white horse. The white horse is in fact the spirit of Eddie's mother who is repeatedly linked in the play with Mary, the suffering mother of Christ. Jim Sheridan's 1993 film, *Into the West*, (which was directed by Mike Newell) also revolves around the figure of a spirit-mother who returns in the form of a white horse to rescue her family from a condition of material and spiritual distress in Dublin's Ballymun Towers.[6] More recently still,

Sinéad O'Connor, one of Ireland's major pop-stars, has been speaking of what she describes as 'Ireland's massive loss of contact with any kind of spirituality'. In an interview in *The Irish Times*, O'Connor argued that this loss of spirituality is part of a general cultural trauma brought about as a result of English conquest, the loss of the Gaelic language, and an attendant loss of a sense of Irish history. Alcoholism and drug addiction, she contended, are symptoms of a general sense of emptiness in contemporary Irish society which can only be overcome by renewing contact with a God whom she preferred to think of as a woman. The unconditional love and compassion of God, O'Connor suggested, are best thought of in maternal terms since: 'A mother is connected to a baby by an umbilical cord; a man is never connected to a baby in that way. God is something that's connected to me no matter what I do' (Interview with Waters, 1). Her 1994 album, *Universal Mother*, O'Connor remarked, represented her attempt to work through her own personal version of the larger cultural traumas referred to.

There is obviously a distinction to be made here between the religious devotee who believes in the actuality of Marian apparition and the invocation of the 'Great Mother' in cultural works such as those of Bolger, O'Connor or Sheridan. That said, however, the fact that a preoccupation with the figure of the 'Great Mother' extends across popular Catholicism into Irish mass culture more generally is a matter of considerable interest in itself. It testifies to what, following Raymond Williams, might be described as the capacity of certain 'structures of feeling' to persist across social institutions and milieus of very different kinds. By 'structures of feeling' Williams refers to way in which meanings and values as they are actively lived and felt are often different from, and sometimes in considerable tension with, people's consciously held formal belief systems (Williams 1977, 132).[7] The concept is useful for this essay insofar as it provides a means to conceptualise how certain forms of religious feeling might persist in cultural works which would not appear to operate within any formally held religious conception of the world.

Bolger's play, Sheridan's film, and Sinéad O'Connor's conception of Irish history all rehearse a curiously similar construction of contemporary Irish reality. In each case a lack is posited at the heart of Irish modernity, and it is this felt sense of lack which then generates an appeal to the figure of the 'Great Mother'. In this essay I want to examine the significance of this construction of things by way of an analysis of Jim Sheridan's *Into the West*. Of the works of mass culture referred to here, Sheridan's makes least overt reference to Catholicism. Precisely because of the distance it preserves from any formalised system of belief, however, the film offers an interesting example of how the meanings and values of a particular 'structure of feeling' can continue to exert a considerable pressure even when translated into a form and idiom quite removed from those with which they are normally associated. The purpose of my analysis of *Into the West*, then, will be to determine the significance of its preoccupation with the figure of the 'Great Mother' in the context of a broader concern with the larger 'structure of feeling' of which the film itself is simply one instance.

II

Given that nineteenth century Anglo-Irish literature had made a very distinctive contribution to the development of the Gothic genre – the names of Maturin, Le Fanu and Stoker being only the most noteworthy in this regard – it might reasonably have been expected that cinematic representations of the supernatural in Ireland would have drawn heavily on this legacy. Strangely, however, cinematic narratives of the 'supernatural Ireland' seem to have avoided the legacy of the Anglo-Irish Gothic romance more or less completely, and to have turned instead for inspiration to the more marvellous literary mode of the fairytale and the folktale. The supernatural in cinematic narratives about Ireland is of a remarkably benign character; it has very little in common with the darker, more sinister worlds of the Gothic romance or the modern occult or horror film. In cinema, the 'supernatural Ireland' has tended to be a world of fairies and leprechauns, not one of vampires and ghouls. In the Gothic mode the supernatural characteristically attaches itself to the claustrophobic interiors and dark declivities of the Big House. In the world of the fairy or folktale, however, stemming perhaps from the pre-capitalist origins of these forms, the supernatural clings to or infuses the open spaces of the landscape itself.[8]

While it is conventional enough to depreciate in aesthetic terms the banality of this cinematic construction of a fairytale Ireland, a more materialist criticism would probably try to explain why cinema should have preferred the Ireland of folk or fairytale to that of the Gothic novel. Part of the answer undoubtedly has to do with the fact that in cinema generally 'Ireland' has come to stand as a veritable signifier of the pre-modern and the anti-modern, its landscape a 'magical' one precisely to the degree that it can be made to stand outside of the world of advanced capitalism. In films such as

Finian's Rainbow or *Darby O'Gill and the Little People*, 'Ireland' becomes a magical landscape suffused with a strong Anglo-American nostalgia for a lost world of the pre-industrial past, a place not yet disenchanted by technological civilisation (the phrase 'the Old Country' should be read as much in terms of modes of production as in terms of emigrant nostalgia). At the risk of stretching things a bit, it might even be argued that this cinematic construction of a fantastic fairytale Ireland is not altogether without affinity, though aesthetically only a poor precursor, to those forms of 'magic realism' (*real maravilloso*) nowadays associated with Latin American and some other 'Third World' cinemas – forms which Fredric Jameson has suggested are constitutively dependent on a content which betrays the overlap or co-existence of pre-capitalist and nascent capitalist modes of production (Jameson 1990, 138). What is curious at any rate is that cinema – the only major art-form to emerge within the world of industrial capitalism – should have provided the most hospitable medium within which the folk and fairytale Ireland of the Irish Literary Renaissance could continue to live on right throughout the twentieth century. In *Celtic Revivals*, Seamus Deane argues that post-Treaty Ireland effectively put an end to the myths of the Irish Literary Revival (Deane 1985, 33). It would be more accurate to say, however, that this mythical Ireland of the Revival did not so much disappear as migrate, moving from the medium of poetry and drama into the more visual medium of cinema where it has since enjoyed a very extended residency indeed. The corollary of cinema's preoccupation with the magical landscape of the Irish Literary Renaissance has been its comparative lack of interest in urban Ireland. Joyce's novelistic mapping of Dublin finds no equivalent in film. Until very recently at least, the city has been notable in cinematic representations of Ireland mostly by its absence.

Jim Sheridan's *Into the West* is a modern fairytale, one which would seem to be a fairly self-conscious of the fact that it is working from within the cinematic tradition just referred to. The film tells the story of how two young traveller brothers who are unhappily settled with their drunken father in Dublin's Ballymun Towers make their escape out of the city and into the rural west of Ireland on a mysterious white horse. The Dublin of the film is very much the degraded urban landscape of romantic convention. It is a decrepit high-rise dystopia where Papa Reilly (Gabriel Byrne), a former 'King of the Travellers', has abandoned the old nomadic ways of his people for the sedentary life of the city. Papa's rejection

of the traditional life of the travellers seems to be driven by the fact
that he blames the 'old ways' for the death of his wife, Mary, a
death with which he has still clearly failed to come to terms.
Although Papa is anxious that his sons, Tito (Ciaran Fitzgerald) and
Ossie (Ruaidhri Conroy), should at least learn to read and write in
order to equip themselves for the modern world, his own continual
drunkenness makes it clear that the transition from the old ways to
the new is a far from successful or happy one. When their grand-
father (David Kelly) arrives in the city accompanied by the mysterious white horse, the younger of the two boys, Ossie, strikes up an
intuitive relationship with the animal which suggests that the
instinctive pull of the old nomadic life continues to exert its force
even in the alien environment of the city. After a series of misad-
ventures in which the horse is impounded by corrupt policemen
and sold illegally to a wealthy County Meath landowner, the two
boys finally recapture the horse and set off westwards across
Ireland with police force and landowner in pursuit.

As the narrative progresses, it becomes increasingly clear to the
audience that it is the mysterious white horse that is really directing
this journey 'into the west'. It also becomes clear that the horse is in
fact the returned spirit of the boys' dead mother, a mother whom
Ossie had never known since she had died giving birth to him. As
this spirit-horse carries the two boys further and further west, Papa,
now searching for his lost sons with the help of some other travellers who have refused to succumb to sedentary life, realises that
the horse is leading him back to the landscape of his own past. The
narrative reaches its climax when the horse eventually reaches the
western coast and, harried on all sides by its pursuers, carries Ossie
out to sea where both boy and horse are submerged beneath the
waves. Just when it seems certain that he must surely drown, Ossie
eventually resurfaces, though not before being granted a vision of
the mother he had never seen. Both father and sons are taken back
into the embrace of the 'unfallen' travelling community and Papa
promises his sons that there will be no returning to their previous
life in the city ('I won't bring ye back to the Towers again, I swear, I
swear'). Clearly the journey on which they have been conducted by
the spirit-mother has been one of psychic and spiritual regeneration, a voyage of rehabilitation which culminates in the rejection of
the city and the alienated mode of existence with which it is associated.

The contrary meanings and values associated with the word
'West' in an Irish context, and a consequent sense of uncertainty as

to what exactly a journey 'into the West' might mean, are what give this narrative its structure. In one obvious sense, the 'West' referred to here is clearly that mythical landscape that has dominated literary representations of the Celtic regions in Europe since at least the nineteenth century. This is the magical 'Celtic west' of Arnold and Renan, a literary construct stretching with remarkable structural consistency from the Celtic exoticism of Ossian and Scott to the Irish Literary Renaissance of Yeats and Synge. As Joseph Leerson has argued, whether the relationship be that between Brittany and France or between Wales and England or between the western and eastern regions of Ireland, this 'Celtic west' is always constructed in terms of an imaginary geography which sets off a materialist, vulgar, modern and mundane 'east' against a dreamy, mystical and timeless 'west'. As Leerson observes: 'The most striking point which such representations have in common is their strongly vectorial bias. They describe not a place, but a direction, a penetration or an approach, a movement from the east to the west, into or towards an unknown Celtic world' (Leerson 1988, 212). For Leerson, this discourse of exoticism describes not so much an arrival as a constant deferral, a quest for the Other Place which always lies somewhere further beyond the horizon.

The irony is, however, that in another less literary and more political register, 'the West' can also mean precisely the opposite of this. In this political register 'the West' refers to the advanced capitalist economies of the modern industrial world, a 'west' virtually synonymous with the United States and Western Europe. This is the advanced industrial Euro-American 'West' into which Ireland as a small, rather helpless economy has become increasingly integrated. The felt experience of that integration is lived as an extremely anxious and threatening one for two reasons: firstly, because its price seems to be increasing political and economic dependency; secondly, because it inevitably threatens the abolition of the traditional, rural Ireland which subtends the exoticism of the other 'Celtic West' which has always furnished the Irish state with its most idealised fantasies of itself. As constructed in Sheridan's film, this political 'West' is represented by the visually drab, spiritually desiccated world of the city. Dublin in the film is a place where one can only live parasitically. We see it first in the form of the Murphys ('the most common name in all Ireland') gathering together their teeming children for the inspection of the social welfare officer. The dominant figure in this landscape is Papa. His drunkenness and craven abjection colours the landscape of the city as a whole. This

'Dublin' is clearly no more a 'real' place than is the 'Celtic West' into which Ossie and Tito flee. It functions in the film as a metaphor for Ireland's problematic position within the economic order of the modern industrial 'west'.

There is, however, a third 'West' in the film, one which complicates the conventional literary binarism already described for us by Leerson. This is the 'Wild West' of Hollywood legend: the cinematic west into which Tito and Ossie like to imagine they are fleeing. It is also the sign within the text which signals that the film knows itself as film. In contrast to the 'Celtic West' which has its origins in the realm of high culture, this 'Wild West' is a product of mass culture, and for the barely literate Ossie and Tito raised in the era of cinema and television it is this celluloid west, rather than its earlier and more indigenous literary counterpart, which structures their fantasy worlds. This cinematic west, however, does not simply co-exist alongside the other two 'Wests' described earlier: in fact it subsumes or colonises both. As the boys flee Dublin and journey into the rural west of Ireland, which for them is an escape into the west of celluloid fantasy, the audience is compelled to recognise that authentic flight from the world of advanced capitalism is no longer really an option if only because this 'flight' is mediated by cinema, and cinema itself of course is both product and instrument of the advanced capitalism that is supposedly being left behind. It may well be possible to leave the city physically behind, but the colonisation of the subconscious by Hollywood and the commodification of landscape by cinema means that the 'West' of advanced capitalism is always one step ahead of one in any event.

This sense of the complicity of cinema and capitalism is necessarily uncomfortable in terms of what it implies both for the future of 'Irish culture' and indeed for the future of cinematic romance. The cinematic romance, like the literary imperial romance which is clearly its precursor, has always translated the world into a western zone of relative order, security and secularity and a non-western world of adventure, magic and disorder. As John McClure has argued, romance is designed to satisfy collective longings for adventure and the exotic. It cannot manufacture its dreams from thin air however: it depends for their production on the existence of regions 'beyond' the pale of civilisation, regions rich in the 'raw materials' of adventure, magic and mystery – regions and populations as yet unconquered and untransformed by the forces of secularisation and rationalisation (McClure 1994, 9: the imaginary geography of Celtic exoticism is clearly just a regional sub-department of this larger romance cartography). As the expansion of advanced capitalism reaches its global limits, however, and the last elsewhere threatens to be eliminated, romance itself inevitably experiences a crisis of the 'raw materials' of magic and mystery on which it had always depended for its existence. The crisis at the centre of Sheridan's *Into the West*, then, is to a large extent a crisis in the production of romance itself since one 'west' (that of advanced capitalism, of which cinema itself is part) effectively obliterates the other 'west' (the rural Ireland which subtended Celtic exoticism) and in so doing deprives romance of its conventional 'raw materials'. To the extent that it is aware of this contradiction, Sheridan's film can be said to be a kind of meta-romance: the journey 'into the west' a desperate quest for the very conditions that make romance possible in a world that seems continually to extend the conditions that make it impossible. But since cinema is itself part of the technological world which is abolishing the conditions on which romance depends, this journey is necessarily an impossible one. Cinema cannot escape the conditions of its own possibility, and even as it appears to flee the world of advanced industrial capitalism it inevitably extends it. Conflating as it does the flight into the 'Celtic West' and 'Wild West', Sheridan's film implicitly acknowledges the impossibility of any real escape; in the world of advanced capitalism the simulacra of escape which is cinema itself is the only 'escape' that remains.[9]

What I have been arguing is that *Into the West* demonstrates a considerable degree of anxiety about the implications of advanced capitalism both in terms of what it means for Ireland generally and, more specifically, for the destruction of the 'raw materials' of romance. Given its acute discomfort with the journey Ireland is making into this political 'west' (that of advanced capitalism) which is also a journey into the future, the film has only one direction to go: into the other 'Celtic west' which is also a journey into the past. At the level of plot at least, this journey into the past would appear to be a wholly therapeutic one. It forces Papa to confront and work through the hitherto unresolved grief that had been at the root of his melancholia, Ossie is granted a vision of the mother he has never known, and the story concludes with the family's reintegration into the larger communal family of the 'unfallen' travellers. In terms which recall Freud's famous essay, 'Mourning and Melancholia', the drama acted out here is one which connects Papa's melancholia with an inability to undertake the 'work of mourning' generated by some trauma in the past – a trauma obviously associated in Sheridan's narrative with the loss of the mother. Read socially, the inference is that Ireland's joyless modernity has something to do with its persistent refusal to come to terms with the traumas of its past – traumas somehow therapeutically worked through by means of the journey into the rural west.

Yet even this particular journey 'into the west' is not without its own anxieties: indeed this turning back to the past cannot avoid suggestions of both psychic and political regression. The 'stresses' of this particular anxiety manifest themselves at several different moments in the narrative. One such moment occurs when Ossie and Tito eventually tire of the hardships of their flight and decide to return to the comforts of the city only to discover that the mysterious white horse has a will of its own and will not allow them to do so. Once embarked upon, the journey 'into the west' appears not to permit of any turning back. Moreover, though the journey eventually does prove regenerative, the film ends happily only after it has first suggested another altogether more disastrous ending during those long moments when it had seemed certain that Ossie must surely drown. The memory of this 'alternative' disastrous ending cannot entirely be expunged by the happy ending with which the narrative 'really' concludes.

It would be wrong to imagine, however, that the anxieties referred to in the previous paragraphs are frontally engaged in the film. They are not. *Into the West* oscillates between a 'disenchanted romanticism', for which capitalism is seen as an irreversible phenomenon which makes it impossible to go back to the pre-industrial past, and a 'past-orientated romanticism', which indeed seeks to return to some civilisational stage before capitalism.[10] Though at one level it acknowledges the futility of its desire, the film ultimately refuses to surrender its dream of returning to the past and its affective loyalties are clearly with the journey into the rural west. For this reason, the anxieties already referred to earlier appear in the film only as points of stress in the narrative or as traces of a certain hesitation or ambivalence. For the most part, however, the film proves quite adept in managing its misgivings, displacing them in all sorts of interesting ways.

As argued earlier, the narrative of *Into the West* operates in terms of a spatialising strategy whereby problems of a socioeconomic character that clearly affect Ireland as a whole are spatially mapped in terms of a geographical division between a mundane, urban east (Dublin) and a magical, rural west. I would argue that what allows Sheridan's narrative to 'contain' whatever misgivings it might have about the regressive implications of the flight from the city into the rural west (which is also the past) is its construction of a third space onto which these misgivings can be projected: 'the midlands'. When Ossie and Tito first escape the city they feel a sense of exhilaration and release. Later, however, they experience hunger, cold and loneliness and Dublin begins to appear more attractive. In moments such as this, the world beyond the city loses its aura of pre-capitalist pastoral arcadia and appears instead as a place of hunger, scarcity and want. The social equivalent of this suggestion that a return to the 'state of nature' might be a return to hardship rather than to a world of natural plenitude occurs in the episode in which Papa and his companions are met with naked anti-traveller prejudice in a small midlands town. That is to say, the space beyond the city is really subdivided into two locales: a sour, provincial 'midlands' which gathers into itself all of the more unattractive implications of a return to the rural past, and a depopulated 'west' free of any such negative associations. The 'midlands' here, it seems to me, functions as a kind of purgative zone where the film's generally suppressed anxieties about the regressive nature of the journey into the past can find open expression; it provides the film with a place where it can, as it were, unload itself of its 'bad conscience' before moving on to the 'west' proper. By affixing onto 'the midlands' what are properly anxieties about the darker implications of its own rejection of the present and its general nostalgia for a return to the rural past, the film manages to retain the fantasy of some pristine west free of any such regressiveness.

Since *Into the West* is a work of romance and not of social realism, it would be a mistake to see the film as one which is in any important sense about the travelling community in Ireland. The travellers in *Into the West* function as the figure of a rather nostalgic desire for a kind of communal collectivity which, in the imagination of the film at least, seems to exist only prior to or outside of the space of the city. Accordingly, the travellers function for the audience as an object of utopian longing for a form of extended family or clan or communal collectivity of the type that is systematically dissolved within the world of advanced capitalism. Commenting on the tremendous popularity of the *Godfather* movies in the United States, Fredric Jameson has observed that the narrative content of these movies is structurally differentiated from earlier paradigms of the gangster movie by its collective nature. Whereas the classical gangster movies of previous eras had constructed the gangster as a lone individual on the edges of society, *The Godfather* took the form of a family or ethnic saga, something which Jameson holds to be an essential part of the film's attraction for a mass audience. For Jameson, ethnic groups in the United States are not only the object of prejudice, but also the object of envy; both impulses are intermingled and mutually reinforce each other. 'The dominant white middle-class groups – already given over to anomie and social fragmentation and atomisation – find in the ethnic and racial groups which are the object of their social repression and status contempt at one and the same time the image of some older collective ghetto or ethnic neighborhood solidarity; they feel the envy and ressentiment of the *Gesellschaft* for the older *Gemeinschaft* which it is simultaneously exploiting and liquidating' (Jameson 1990, 33). This, it seems to me, describes exactly the function of the travellers in *Into the West* and indeed in Sheridan's earlier film *The Field*. Part neither of the social atomisation of the city nor of the social isolation of the countryside, the travellers in these films represent a utopian desire for a form of communal collectivity that would escape the characteristic constraints of both town and country living alike.[11]

Even though the travellers fulfil the same structural function in *Into the West* and *The Field* as the Italian mafia-family do in the *Godfather* films, they clearly represent a nostalgia for a collectivity of a very different kind. Whereas the mafia of the *Godfather* movies are a complex composite of the value-worlds of American big business and Sicilian feudalism, the travellers in Sheridan's work function as a fantasy of a much simpler and more idyllic pre-capitalist community. Sheridan's travellers are nomadic wanderers who seem to exist outside of the sedentary world of fixed property relations altogether; vestiges of a primeval animism and pagan magic cling to them. Tito tells Ossie ruefully that the travellers of old could 'tell fortunes, make things out of tin, do magic'. Driving the film's nostalgia for the travellers, therefore, would appear to be a form of romantic anti-capitalism of the kind that idealises primitive artisan production or some even older primitive communist society of the remote past.

There is one other striking difference between the mafia-family in the *Godfather* movies and Sheridan's travellers. Whereas the mafia-family in the *Godfather* movies suggests a nostalgia for a tightly integrated family or kinship unit presided over by the fearsome yet reassuring authority of a God-Father figure, the pre-capitalist 'traveller community' in *Into the West* is presided over by a Spirit-Mother. That this pre-capitalist community is imagined as a matriarchate is confirmed by the fact that it is the returned spirit of the dead mother that lures her 'fallen' family out of the city and takes it on a journey that will draw it back into the past and into the embrace of the larger community of their unfallen kin. Moreover, though the unsettled travellers seem nominally to be ruled over by a male, Tracker (Johnny Murphy), real authority proves ultimately to lie with his sister Kathleen (Ellen Barkin). It is Kathleen, and not Tracker, who takes on the task of helping Papa to track his boys. In her role as guide on this journey 'into the west' she becomes in effect the living surrogate of the spirit mother who really presides over the journey. Inscribing a trajectory from centre out to periphery, from the capital city of the 'fallen' father to the western ocean of maternality, *Into the West* is a fantasy about a return to the world of the archaic mother, the pre-oedipal mother who comes long before the appearance of the father and the distinctions and hierarchies that the law-of-the-father inaugurates. The trajectory inscribed in the narrative is one consistent with conventional literary archetypes in which the father represents the hard jural line of authority and property transmission, while the mother represents the affectional, soft side, providing sanctuary and harmony.

Now in one sense this desire for a form of community presided over by the Spirit-Mother is clearly part of an even broader desire on the part of the narrative for a return to some 'original state of nature' that would also be a return to some imaginary time before either class or gender hierarchies. This is the positive or utopian dimension of the film: unable to see any end to the capitalist present which is obviously not to its liking, the film tries to reach back for a glimpse of a more primeval past before capitalism even begins. In another sense, however, it is also the case that it is precisely this utopian strand in the film which functions as what Jameson might call the fantasy bribe that the work of mass culture must always feed to the audience it is about ideologically to manipulate (Jameson 1990, 25). It is after all the construction of the journey into the past as a return to some more 'feminine' or 'maternal' world that chiefly enables the film to ward off, or at least to hold at arm's length, the suspicion that its desire to go back to the past is a politically regressive one. If there is one constituency in contemporary Ireland for whom the prospect of a journey into the past will surely have least appeal, then it is women – a constituency for whom the past can mostly be expected to appear as a long chronicle of oppressions and discriminations. The only thing that enables the film, then, to maintain the aura of visual and emotional attractiveness in which it steeps the past is its construction of that past – in deliberate misrecognition of all historical evidence to the contrary – as a time-space which is somehow more 'maternal', more authentically instinct or vibrant with the 'feminine' than the present. (It is characteristic of the general ambivalence of this film, however, that even in this respect it cannot altogether dispel the darker side of the past to which it nonetheless insists on returning. Moreover, this darker side of the past insinuates itself into the narrative specifically as a memory of female suffering. In her earlier human incarnation, the spirit-mother in the film had died in childbirth, a death Papa associates with traveller 'superstition' and the concomitant refusal to come to terms with the modern.)

It is no doubt precisely the difficulty of constructing the journey into the past as a return to a more maternal world that necessitates that the mother appear in the film in supernatural form. Were she to be present as living wife and mother, it would obviously be much more difficult to represent the journey into the past as a voyage into a more 'feminine' world in a credible manner. Given the nature of the narrative, then, the mother can only appear in the film as a supernatural presence: as a vague signifier of some previous state that is never named, as that oceanic thing that calls for fusion. It is no accident in this context that the living woman, Kathleen, is sexually unattached in the film: skirting the issue of sexual relations allows the film to maintain its edenic conception of the past as a place innocent of conventional sexual organisation and hierarchy.

As I interpret it, then, *Into the West* is a film marked by a passionate rejection of Ireland's capitalist modernity. That rejection is complicated, rather than ameliorated, by the film's uneasy self-consciousness that cinema itself is one of the crucial technologies of the modern world which the film rejects. Since its view of this capitalist modernity is an unremittingly bleak and negative one – it is unable to locate any seeds of resistance to the present condition of things within the city itself – the film inevitably turns its back on this modern world and looks for a redemptive alternative in an idealised version of the premodern, pre-capitalist past. The choice between these two worlds is inscribed in the narrative in terms of a familiar romantic cartography which divides the world into two zones: one modern and urban, secularised and spiritually dry; the other pre-modern and rural, a place still vibrant with wonder, magic, and spiritual experience. The return to this latter zone is constructed as a return to a condition of pre-oedipal oneness with the archaic mother, a condition that the child experiences as an undifferentiated unity where all its needs are provided for. The narrative trajectory of the film functions, therefore, by superimposing three parallel quests upon each other: a quest for the maternal world of childhood (Ossie's search for the lost mother he cannot remember); a quest for the historical childhood of humankind (Papa's abandonment of the city and return to 'the old ways'); and the film's own need to imagine a space not yet disenchanted by the forces of rationalisation and progress, a space where the raw materials of romance might still be found. The desire for the lost homeland of maternality which drives the utopian impulses of the film entails, however, a rather obvious forgetting of the darker and more oppressive aspects of the past to which it looks for redemption. It entails an active forgetting, that is, of all of the hardships and shortcomings of the past that have spurred the development of our capitalist modernity in the first instance.

III

It will be clear by now that we have not left the world of Knock behind. Though in Sheridan's film she seems to belong more to the realm of pagan animism than to Catholicism proper, the spirit-mother in *Into the West* functions in a manner which closely resembles that of the Madonna in Marian apparitions. She even bears the name of the Madonna and there are several allusions in the film which link the two figures.[12] The crucial resemblance, however, has to do less with these allusions and more with the organisational function of the mother figure within the larger framework of the narrative. What Sheridan's film offers its audience is an essentially pessimistic vision of a 'fallen' modernity, a world of mourning and melancholia, redeemed only by the supernatural intervention of the spirit-mother. That the film reaches towards an essentially religious experience of the numinous is suggested by the fact that the regenerative journey 'into the west' reaches its apotheosis when Ossie is granted an epiphanic vision of the spirit-mother. In Sheridan's film, as in the Marian apparition at Knock, the spirit-mother functions both as a silent figure of admonition (serving as the warning which finally persuades Papa to forsake 'new ways' and return to the 'old ways' of the tribe) and as a figure of enormous consolation (reassuring Ossie that he has not after all been abandoned in a cold and heartless world). In *Into the West*, as in the messages conventionally associated with Marian apparitions, salvation is to be found by 'turning back' from the fallen present to some supposedly simpler and more spiritual past.

This is not to argue that *Into the West* consciously functions as a religious fiction. A nostalgic valorisation of the mother and a desire for the homeland of lost maternality is a constitutive feature of a whole range of Irish political discourses whether of a religious, nationalist, socialist, feminist or ecological kind, and the construct of the maternal in *Into the West* may well owe as much to one or other of these discourses as to Catholicism. In fact, one of the more curious and telling things about *Into the West* is the facility with which it will lend itself to a reading in terms of any one of the discourses just referred to. As well as the 'socialistic' or 'religious' impulses which co-exist alongside each other in the narrative, the film will also lend itself to a 'feminist' reading as a fable about the need to renew contact with some feminine principle perceived as exiled from a patriarchal world, as an 'ecological' fable about the need to return to some more natural state of existence, or even as a 'nationalist' fable about the need for the nation to return to some more authentic course from which it has strayed.

The problem here is not that there are as many interpretations as there are interpretative methods. The recurrent mythologisation of the mother – whether as Madonna in Catholicism, Kathleen Ni Houlihan in nationalism, feminist attempts to retrieve the Great Goddess, the Mother Earth of the ecologists, or even socialism's matriarchal era of prehistory – can be explained, I believe, by the fact that in their more populist versions all of these discourses tend to slide into one or other of the modalities of romantic anti-capitalism – one of the most deeply rooted and consistent forces in Irish political culture throughout the past century.[13] By romantic anti-capitalism I mean that running across all of these different discourses is a critique, no matter how feebly developed, of advanced capitalist society – a critique elaborated not from the stand-point of the future, however, but from that of an idealised version of some pre-capitalist past. If the film proves amenable to the various readings referred to in the previous paragraph, then this is because in their more populist forms all of these discourses can become variants of a general romantic anti-capitalist 'structure of feeling' and can share a common libidinal economy, however much they may be at odds with each other on other levels.

Since in all of these discourses the 'Great Mother' is associated with the idealised past, the audience's identification with her serves to direct its desire away from the future where the discontents of the present might be redressed by the construction of some better order of things. This structuration of desire amounts to a retreat from the undoubtedly formidable challenges of our present capitalist modernity. By locating what can only be realised exclusively in the future as that which has already existed in the past, this retrospective-oriented mode of thought, as Mikhail Bakhtin has observed in a memorable phrase, effectively 'empties out the future, dissects and bleeds it white as it were' (Bakhtin 1981,148).

Clearly this particular structuration of desire has political implications. The retrospective orientation of the various forms of romantic anti-capitalism is such that they have rarely generated anything more than a sentimental critique of capitalism. A more rigorous and dialectical critique of the shortcomings of capitalist modernity must necessarily be articulated, however, by measuring capitalism not against the ruins of the past, but against the demands and the as-yet-unrealised possibilities of the future. The point made here is hardly new, but the persistence and indeed the contemporary resurgence of romantic anti-capitalism in all of its various manifestations requires that it be reiterated nonetheless. Commenting on the romanticism of the Russian Narodniks, Lenin acknowledged that the 'wishes of the romanticists are very good' and that their 'recognition of the contradictions of capitalism places them above the blind optimists who deny the existence of these contradictions' (Lenin 1960, 242). Lenin also insisted, however, that the nature of the romantic critique of capitalism meant that the actual policies of the romanticists could never be effective in practice since they amounted to little more than a futile demand for the retardation of capitalist development rather than for its revolutionary transformation. However unfashionable it may be to cite Lenin in our present moment in history, the validity of this critique of romantic anti-capitalism has not diminished.

Just as the nostalgia for pre-capitalist worlds is generally unproductive in the context of socialism's larger project, so too the spiritualisation of the mother has generally functioned as more of a hindrance than a help to feminism's larger project. As Jan Relf has argued, constructions of the mother as some theistic oceanic or earth force elevate motherhood to the status of the mystical, perpetuate unhelpfully essentialist beliefs about an 'innate' female nature, and reinforce long-standing metaphorical associations which collapse any distinctions between 'women' and 'nature' (Relf 1993, *passim*). In her analysis of the cult of the Virgin Mother in Catholicism, Julia Kristeva has written that: 'Man overcomes the unthinkable of death by postulating maternal love in its place – in the place and stead of death and thought' (Kristeva 1986, 176). For

Kristeva, the traditional consecration of motherhood, whether religious or secular, involves less an idealisation of the archaic mother 'than the idealisation of the relationship that binds us to her – an idealisation of primary narcissism' (161). Behind this idealising process, then, Kristeva argues, is an anguished desire for an escape from the demands of representation and the symbolic altogether. If the desire for the 'Great Mother' and for some pre-capitalist 'state of nature' so often go hand in hand with each other, this is undoubtedly because both participate in this same process of primary narcissism.

A point usefully emphasised by Kristeva, however, is that it is insufficient simply to declaim against traditional constructs of the maternal since this may be to fail to recognise or merely to circumvent the real experiences to which such constructs attempt, however unsatisfactorily, to respond. Keeping this in mind, it has to be recognised that if the figure of the 'Great Mother' continues to persist in contemporary Irish culture then this is not just because of some unfortunate historical 'hangover' from the past, or because of the continuing power of Catholicism, but because the appeal to the figure of the 'Great Mother' continues to have its roots in real social conflicts and in the tensions generated by those conflicts. In a present lived as tension between the desire for some more natural, human way of living and the objective demands of the country's ongoing integration into a global capitalist economy, the appeal to the 'Great Mother' registers both a longing for some more harmonious order of things and a rather despairing cry for consolation. The more 'otherworldly' or 'supernatural' the Mother appealed to, the more despairing the discourse since the corollary of the appeal to the supernatural is a corresponding lack of confidence that genuine change can be effected by human agency.

It is usually assumed that the appeal of the 'Great Mother' in Irish culture has its sources in the traumas of the past. Conquest, colonisation, famine, the loss of the Gaelic language, and so on are often cited in this context. This appeal to the traumas of the past, however, is only another way of deflecting attention away from the traumas of the present which are always more difficult to confront. The real trauma which ultimately lies behind contemporary Irish culture's preoccupation with the haunting figure of the 'Great Mother' – whether in Sheridan's *Into the West*, Dermot Bolger's *One Last White Horse* or Sinéad O'Connor's *Universal Mother* – is the failure of the Left to articulate a compelling vision of an alternative to the existing order of things. Since modern utopian thought has been so closely associated with socialism of one kind or another, the much proclaimed 'death of socialism' in recent years has resulted in a situation in which contemporary society finds itself without belief in or vision of a future which will be radically better than the present. In the space opened up by the set-backs experienced by the Left, religious and romantic critiques of our capitalist modernity can be expected to step in to try to fill the void. It is this loss of confidence in the possibility of realising a world radically better than the present, and not the traumas of the past, which explains why the anguished appeal to the love of the 'Great Mother' continues to resonate in contemporary Irish culture.

Notes

1. In his splendid analysis of the early years of cinema in Europe, Noel Burch contends that the Catholic Church was conscious from the very start that cinema was a dangerous rival (Burch 1990, 77-79n1). Burch cites a 1904 passage from the French Catholic magazine, *Le Fascinateur*, which gives an account of the fascination of a Parisian audience with the spectacle of cinematography. The disapproving author of this article clearly conceives of the crowd's fascination with cinematography as a kind of 'false' or degraded version of a religious experience of the miraculous:

> In the evenings, on our main boulevards, traffic is halted by a stupid throng of gawpers who stand around for hours, their feet in the mud, their noses in the air, their eyes turned upward, jostled, trampled, indifferent to their own concerns and to how ridiculous they look, hypnotised by the magical screen set up on top of a five-storey building and resplendent with some wretched figures of advertisements. *Before these luminous apparitions the crowd is in ecstasy, and Parisians take on the air of illuminati.* We should not be surprised at this naïve passion. It is so natural to mankind! (Burch 77-78n13, emphasis mine)

Burch points out, however, that the various churches did not simply react against cinema, but were also among the first to discover the usefulness of projected pictures, and to deploy them in the joint struggle against the secularisation and alcoholism of the working classes.

2. It is perhaps a mark of the infancy of Irish film criticism that, insofar as the topic has received any attention at all, the question of the

relationship between church and cinema in Ireland has been conceived of almost exclusively in terms of censorship. Though this topic is certainly important, construction of the relationship between church and cinema exclusively in terms of censorship inevitably tends to pit the two as polarised antagonists. All of the more complex ways in which church and cinema compete with and indeed cooperate with each other tend to be flattened out in such analyses.

3. Turner observes that: 'Since 1830 ... there has been a marked increase in Marian apparitions, increasingly associated with warnings of dire calamities to be visited on mankind if it does not repent and mend its ways – a kind of Catholic millenarianism' (*Image and Pilgrimage*, 149). He also notes that: 'The nineteenth century and the first half of the twentieth century have constituted what has been called, in Catholic circles, the Age of Mary' (208).

4. In her analysis of the matriarchate, Fluehr-Lobban notes that in none of Marx's writings on primitive communist societies is there any suggestion that he accepted the historical priority of the matriarchate. Fluehr-Lobban cites Marx's comment that: 'The recollection of a prior state of greater freedom and influence in the position of women accounts for one half of the mythology of Juno and Minerva. The other half of the account is that projection into heaven of the ancient freedom and equality of women is the inversion of their actual position in Greek society; it is also justification in the mythology of their constraint in that low position, and the expression of a hopeful fantasy of its betterment in another world' (Fluehr-Lobban, 344). Marx's reservation about the notion of the matriarchate is in keeping with his approach to the idea of primitive communism which was generally more circumspect than that of Engels.

5. It should be clear that I am not referring here to all forms of socialist thought or to all forms of feminist thought and so on. Just as the idealisation of pre-capitalist societies is antithetical to most forms of socialist thought, so too the attempt to recuperate a female deity is obviously antithetical to many forms of feminism and is mostly associated with 'radical feminism'. A preoccupation with the 'Great Mother' is a recurrent feature in women's utopian fiction.

6. *Into the West*, a Littlebird production made with the participation of British Screen, was directed by Mike Newell and written by Jim Sheridan (based on a story by Michael Pearce). Since Newell came late to the production, I have departed from the usual convention whereby 'authorship' of a film is generally attributed to its director.

Although for reasons of convenience, therefore, the film is described hereafter as Sheridan's, the collaborative nature of its production and its multiple authorship are assumed throughout. Indeed, I will argue later in the essay that the nostalgia expressed in *Into the West* for a more authentic Irish past sits uneasily with an awareness in the film of the increasingly transnationalised nature of cinematic production. This generates a certain tension or ambivalence which manifests itself throughout the narrative of this film.

7. Defining the terms 'structure of feeling', Williams writes that:

> The term is difficult, but 'feeling' is chosen to emphasise a distinction from more formal concepts of 'world-view' or 'ideology'. It is not only that we must go beyond formally held and systematic beliefs, though of course we have always to include them. It is that we are concerned with meanings and values as they are actively lived and felt, and the relations between these and formal or systematic beliefs are in practice variable (including historically variable), over a range from formal assent with private dissent to the more nuanced interaction between selected and interpreted beliefs and acted and justified experiences ... We are talking about characteristic elements of impulse, restraint, and tone; specifically affective elements of consciousness and relationships: not feeling against thought, but thought as felt and feeling as thought: practical consciousness of a present kind, in a living and inter-relating continuity. We are then defining these elements as a 'structure': as a set, with specific internal relations, at once interlocking and in tension (*Marxism and Literature*, 132).

8. In Robert Wynne-Simmons' *The Outcasts* (1982) the supernatural is a much darker force than in many cinematic representations of the supernatural in Ireland. Even in this film, however, the supernatural is associated with the primeval forces of nature and landscape. The supernatural, that is to say, belongs to the world 'outside' of the domestic enclosure of the house.

9. My suggestion that the conflict between the expansion of technolgical civilisation and the elimination of the conventional 'raw materials' of romance is a preoccupation in *Into the West* is confirmed by several citations in the film. The most obvious perhaps is the fact that at one stage in the film we watch a settled traveller family watching a television screening of *Butch Cassidy and the Sundance Kid*, a classic narrative about the closing of the American frontier – one of the decisive moments in the 'crisis in romance' referred to here.

10. In 'Marxism and Revolutionary Romanticism' Michael Lowy provides a very succinct account of the various modalities of romantic anti-capitalism. According to Lowy, a nostalgia for the pre-capitalist past is a constitutive feature of all forms of romanticism. A 'past-orientated' or 'retrograde' romanticism is one which seeks to re-establish an earlier social state – the past in question may vary, however, from the Catholic Middle Ages to some form of primitive communist society. A 'disenchanted romanticism' is one which recognises the irreversibilty of capitalist society though capitalism may be viewed as a cultural decline from some earlier state. Lowy associates turn-of-the-century German sociologists such as Tonnies or Weber with 'disenchanted romanticism'.

11. That an anxiety about social atomisation is indeed the reverse side of the film's drive to recover some older form of collectivity is confirmed by one of the most spectacular scenes in *Into the West*. In the scene in question the Gardaí arrive to impound the white horse which Ossie and Tito have brought into their Ballymun apartment. In the melée that follows the panicked horse kicks a massive hole in the wall which partitions off the Reillys' apartment from that of their neighbours who are sitting huddled around their television set. The horse here represents a natural force which breaks down the 'unnatural' barriers that isolate people by boxing them off from each other into isolated compartments. Ironically, however, Tito, who has been banned from watching television in his own apartment, later uses the gaping hole in the wall to watch the neighbours' television. The ubiquity of television – the real 'hole in the wall' through which so many attempt to escape the alienation and isolation of advanced capitalist society – is thus acknowledged even as the film tries to escape it.

12. On their journey westwards the two boys stop to pray before a statue of the Blessed Virgin. In another scene, Papa enters the caravan where he had lived with Mary before her death and looks at her photograph against a background which features a picture of the Blessed Virgin.

13. Although the subject of romanticism in Irish culture has certainly received considerable scholarly attention, a comprehensive analysis of Irish romantic anti-capitalism has still to be produced. The development of such an analysis has been impeded perhaps by the tendency to frame the subject in a narrowly aestheticist and Anglocentric frame of reference. Whereas Irish romanticism is usually analysed with reference to its English counterpart, it may well have

more in common with other more politically influential strands of romantic anti-capitalism in other industrially backward parts of the world. Whereas romanticism in Britain and France appeared in industrially advanced metropolitan societies, Irish romanticism might more appropriately be compared with that of the Narodniks in Russia or the Gandhists in India, both peripheral, industrially underdeveloped and overwhelmingly agricultural societies like Ireland.

Bibliography

Bachofen, Johann Jacob, *Das Mutterrecht*, Stuttgart 1861.

Bakhtin, Mikhail, *The Dialogic Imagination*, U of Texas P, Austin 1981.

Bolger, Dermot, *One Last White Horse*, in *A Dublin Quartet*, Penguin Books, Harmondsworth 1992.

Burch, Noel, *Life to those Shadows*, BFI Publishing (Woodstock Books), London 1990.

Deane, Seamus, *Celtic Revivals*, Faber and Faber, London 1985.

Engels, Frederick, *The Origin of the Family, Private Property and the State* (1891), International Press, New York 1972.

Fluehr-Lobban, Carolyn, 'A Marxist Reappraisal of the Matriarchate', *Current Anthropology*, 20/2 (June 1979), 341-48.

Freud, Sigmund, 'Mourning and Melancholia', in Philip Rieff, ed., *General Psychological Theory*, MacMillan, New York 1976.

Jameson, Frederic, *Signatures of the Visible*, Routledge, New York and London 1990.

Kristeva, Julia, 'Stabat Mater', in Toril Moi, ed., *The Kristeva Reader*, Basil Blackwell, Oxford 1986, 160-86.

Leerson, Joseph Th., 'Outward Bound: The Locale And Ontology Of Cultural Stereotype In The Case Of Celtic Exoticism', in Roger Bauer et al., eds., *Proceedings of the XIIth Congress Of The International Comparative Literature Association*, Vol 4, Iudicium Verlag, München 1990, 212-16.

Lenin, V. I., 'A Characterisation of Economic Romanticism', *Collected Works*, Vol 2, 1895-1897, Foreign Language Publishing House, Moscow 1960, 133-265.

Lowy, Michael, 'Marxism and Revolutionary Romanticism', *Telos*, 49 (Fall 1981), 83-95.

McClure, John, *Late Imperial Romance*, Verso, London and New York 1994.

Relf, Jan, 'Utopia the Good Breast: Coming Home to Mother', in Krishan Kumar and Stephen Bann, eds., *Utopias and the Millennium*, Reaktion Books, London 1993, 107-28.

Turner, Victor, *Image and Pilgrimage in Christian Culture*, Basil Blackwell, Oxford 1978.

Waters, John, 'Sinéad The Keener', *The Irish Times* (Jan 28, 1995), Weekend 1-2.

Warner, Marina, *Alone Of All Her Sex*, Picador, London 1985.

Williams, Raymond, 'Structures of Feeling', in *Marxism and Literature*, Oxford UP, Oxford 1977, 128-35.

Contributors

JOE CLEARY received an M.A. in English in Maynooth in 1986. In 1991 he received an M.Phil at Columbia University, New York, where he is currently completing his Ph.D dissertation on the subject of partition and narrative form in Ireland, India and Palestine. Research interests include Colonial and Postcolonial Studies, Renaissance Literature, and Literary Theory. His 'Theory in the Age of Mechanical Annihilation' appeared in *Textual Practice* (1992).

BRIAN COSGROVE: Having taught for many years at University College, Dublin, Brian Cosgrove came to Maynooth as Head of the English Department in 1992. His publications include *Wordsworth and the Poetry of Self-Sufficiency* (1982). He has a special interest in the application of theological speculation to literature.

PETER DENMAN: Has written about nineteenth-century fiction and about Irish poetry, including a book *Samuel Ferguson: The Literary Achievement* (1990).

RICHARD HAYES: Lectures both in Maynooth and in the Mater Dei Institute of Education, Dublin. He has published an index to *Poetry Ireland Review* and has written a number of essays and reviews on contemporary Irish literature. He is co-editor (with Dr Chris Morash) of a collection of essays on The Famine, due to be published in late-1995, and the assistant Irish Editor of the *Irish Literary Supplement*. His research interests include contemporary Irish poetry, contemporary fiction, and seventeenth-century English literature.

ANGELA M. LUCAS: Lecturer in English at St Patrick's College Maynooth, teaching Medieval Literature. She is the author of *Women in the Middle Ages: Religion Marriage and Letters*, and *Anglo-Irish Poems of the Middle Ages*, published in this Maynooth Bicentenary Series.

SÉAMUS MACGABHANN: Formerly Deputy Director of Journalism, Dublin Institute of Technology. Subsequently lecturer in Irish and English and Acting Head of the English Department, Carysfort College of Education. Research interests include the influence of Irish language literature, folklore and culture on Anglo-Irish literature and language; the poetry of Seamus Heaney. Editor of the journal *Ríocht na Midhe*.

FRANK MCGUINNESS: One of the leading contemporary Irish dramatists, his works include *Observe the Sons of Ulster Marching towards the Somme* (published 1986), *Carthaginians* (1988), and *Someone Who'll Watch Over Me* (1922), which ran successfully on Broadway as well as in London and Dublin. A collection of poetry, *Booterstown*, was published in 1994.

CHRIS MORASH is the author of *Writing the Irish Famine* (Oxford, 1995). He has edited a collection of Famine poetry, *The Hungry Voice* (Dublin, 1989), and is currently co-editing an interdisciplinary collection of essays on the Famine. He has published a number of essays on nineteenth-century Irish writing and Irish theatre, and has contributed to reference works including the *Oxford Companion to Irish Literature*, *Blackwell's Companion to Irish Culture* and the *World Encyclopedia of Contemporary Theatre*. He was born in Canada and educated at Trinity College, Dublin.